Advance Praise for UN

MW00529645

"A gem of a book in the genre of 'Nature is God's art.' O'Casey paints a rich portrait of nature, verdant with rich hues of biology, with undertones of scripture and wonderment. Her use of metaphors that link the nuances of nature to our spiritual growth makes this a self-enriching treasure and a wonderful book for meaningful group studies. This is not your typical tiring overly-detailed naturalist guide but one that lets us rejoice in admiration of God artistry."

–Kim Patten, Ph.D, professor, Washington State University

"From the perspective of a person who has always been fascinated by the details of nature (God's design and workmanship are astounding), I recommend this book to anyone who needs to slow down and be reminded of this amazing planet we get to live on."

–Michele R. Myers, photographer, hiker, nature enthusiast, BA in Environmental Studies

"Carol O'Casey beckons us to consider the wonders of God's creation. To savor, to relish, to partake, to revel in: in this hurried life do we make the time to do such things? Take up the challenge. Each chapter is an event well worth it. Open yourself to a greater sense of the Creator who loves you so much. Take the time to read and interact in this most unique book."

–Dennis Ellingson, author of GOD'S HEALING HERBS and GOD'S WILD HERBS

Unwrapping WONDER

Unwrapping WONDER

Finding Hope in the Gift of Nature

CAROL O'CASEY

CLADACH
Publishing

Unwrapping Wonder: Finding Hope in the Gift of Nature

Published by CLADACH PUBLISHING PO Box 336144 Greeley, CO 80633
www.cladach.com

Printed in the United States of America

Library of Congress Cataloging-in-Publication Data
O'Casey, Carol, 1959-
Unwrapping wonder : finding hope in the gift of nature / by Carol O'Casey.
pages cm
Includes bibliographical references.
ISBN 978-0-9818929-8-6 -- ISBN 0-9818929-8-1
1. Nature--Religious aspects. 2. Philosophy of nature. 3. Wonder. 4. Hope.
I. Title.
BT695.5.O275 2013
242--dc23
2013015311

Acknowledgments

First and foremost, I thank God who created me with a passion for his creation.

I am also indebted to my family, who believed in me when I did not believe in myself.

To my husband, Terry: I am grateful for your constant love and unwavering support. It is a joy to journey through life with you.

To my children: my daughter Elizabeth, who insisted I write this book and painstakingly edited the first draft; and Michael, Emily, and Isaac who encouraged me each step of the way; thank you from the bottom of my heart. I am blessed to have each of you in my life.

To my extended family: kudos to my sister Colleen who saw me through the daily "chop-wood, carry-water" drudgery of the writing process; my aunt Marilyn who shared her wisdom and writing advice; my brother Kevin, who demonstrated the ability to endure when life is tough; and to my dear mother, Virginia, my soul sister and friend, who put up with my childhood years of harboring crickets, hermit crabs, and lizards in my room and loved me anyway.

Special thanks to Dr. Kim Patten who gave me the opportunity to conduct research in the wild beauty of Willapa Bay. I'm also grateful to the researchers and scholars whose data I have cited in the text. Any errors in interpretation of the data are mine alone.

Finally, I want to express gratitude to my publisher, Catherine Lawton, who believed in my idea and worked tirelessly to see it through to publication; to Matt, whose detailed drawings add clarity and dimension to *Unwrapping Wonder;* and to my editors, Christina Slike and Catherine Lawton, who with their sharp editing eyes helped me whittle *Wonder* into a smoother, more satisfying version for you, my dear reader.

Contents

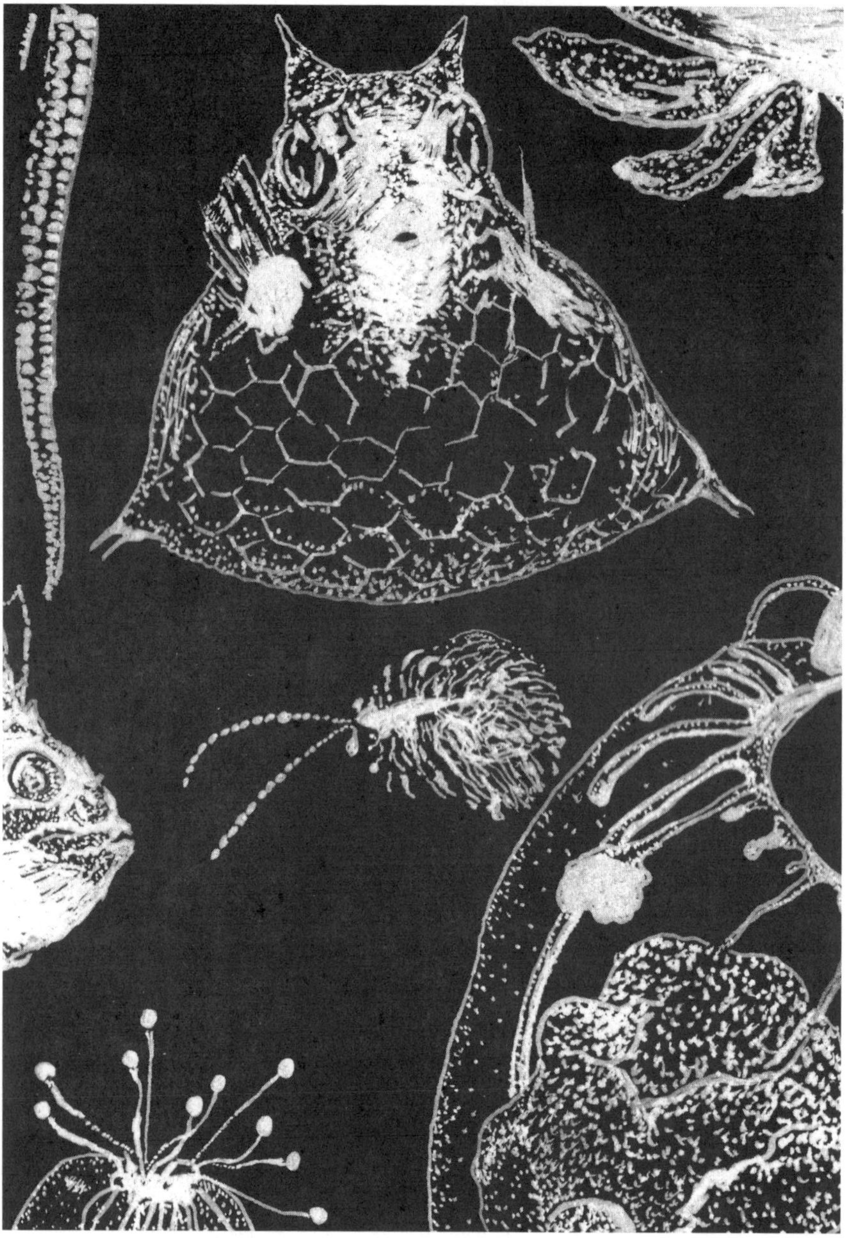

GETTING STARTED
Rediscovering Wonder

I was born to be wild. As soon as I could walk, I toddled outdoors and explored nature's wonders. I unzipped feathers, watched tadpoles knit themselves into frogs and studied skies of quilted clouds. I was at home in nature. Connecting it all to God would come later. Much later.

Those childhood years as an amateur naturalist fueled my passion for nature and led me to pursue a degree in marine biology. Yet, somewhere in the middle of a hardcore science education, I met a man studying to be a pastor. Who says God doesn't have a sense of humor? Suddenly my world of science collided with the world of religion. Little did I know I would soon become a biologist and a pastor's wife.

Yet life as a pastor's wife never quite fit. I felt like a square peg in a round holy. I spent years living as a frustrated field biologist stuffed in the skin of a pastor's wife—that stereotypic role which conjures up a choir-singing, piano-playing prim and properly dressed soul leading a charge of women in all things churchy. That's not me. I prefer God's natural world.

While God doesn't promise us a life of comfort, he does promise to walk beside us. So I navigated the road of the ministry, rough edges and all. Along the way, God provided rich rest stops that soothed my soul. I found hope in his gift of nature as I escaped the expectations of ministry and took a walk on the wild side. Whether exploring field or forest, marsh or meadow, or the edge of the sea, in the natural world I was transformed. There, in the solitude of nature I experienced God's presence.

What about you? Are you burdened with expectations? Do you feel drained from the demands of the day? God's creation has the power to restore wonder. And wonder connects us with the divine.

Renowned agricultural researcher George Washington Carver experienced awe in his encounters with the natural world and exclaimed,

> I love to think of nature as unlimited broadcasting stations, through which God speaks to us every day, every hour and every moment of our lives, if we will only tune in...[1]

In a society obsessed with speed, we must slow down, tune in. How often during an average day do you tune in—or tune out? What daily distractions can scramble your signal?

Perhaps Moses, the ancient futurist, could be considered the pioneer of tuning in to the God frequency. Moses was a murder convict on the lam, wandering in the wilderness, when he stumbled upon wonder. He could have missed the whole shebang. I'm thankful he didn't. Consider Moses's journey en route to wonder:

Moses sees: To avoid murder charges and Pharaoh's pursuit, Moses escapes to the wilderness. While tending the sheep on the far side of the desert (read: the middle of nowhere) Moses sees a sight that piques his curiosity: "Moses saw that though the bush was on fire, it did not burn up" (Exodus 3:2).

Moses slows: Moses moves into step two of his journey to wonder as he intentionally veers off course and investigates. In our frantic, time-starved lives, we often fail to notice what we are seeing. Not Moses. Moses, in the act of holy wondering, pursues this sight of wonder. This burning bush intrigues him and he desires to know more.

Granted, this is probably easy for him to do. After all, what else do you do in a desert in the days of pre-Kindle, pre-wireless internet, pre-cell phones, pre-modern conveniences that, while helpful on one front, distract us from the wonder of nature on the other. Moses entertains himself with the world around him—in this case, a burning bush that does not stop. I guess he had become tired of counting sheep (sorry; couldn't resist).

Moses connects: Because Moses slows to see, he experiences step three on the journey to wonder: Moses connects in a conversation with the God of the universe. "When the Lord saw that he had gone over to look..." (Exodus 3:4). Whoa. Let's just park there for a minute. Did you catch that? God was watching him the whole time!

God was watching and waiting to see what Moses would do with this wonder created to catch his attention. Imagine God, in eager anticipation, peering out from behind the curtain of his magnificence, waiting to see how Moses would respond. Would Moses look? Would he divert his attention from his everyday duties to notice this amazing sight sparked into existence especially for him? He did.

What happens next dazzles the mind. God calls to him from within the bush, "Moses! Moses!" And so begins a personal conversation with the Creator of the universe. How amazing. While Moses leads the sheep through a wasteland of wilderness, dutifully engaged in the ho-hum routine of life, the Creator of the cosmos calls to him. God calls to Moses the murderer, Moses the runaway, Moses the coward hiding in the desert.

Let's be real. There is no hiding from God. When God wants us, he finds us. His presence goes before us, wherever we go. His presence waits for our attention.

Notice how Moses responds to God: "Here I am." Three simple words. Honest. Concise. To the point. Through wonder, the burning bush is seared into Moses's mind; God gets his attention and Moses is ready to listen. No excuses (those come later). Perhaps Moses is stunned speechless. I know I would be. What would be your response to such a call?

"Great are the works of the Lord; they are pondered by all who delight in them" (Psalm 111:2). As a "wonderologist" (one who studies the wonders of nature), I delight in the details of nature. From the bumblebee that manages to fly on wings that appear too small for its ungainly body; to the dragonfly that rises from its waterlogged larval form and morphs to a powerful airborne adult; to the barnacle, that literally stands on its head and snatches its meals with its legs, God entertains and delights us with the endless wonders he has created.

Now I confess, I've never seen a burning bush; but then, I'm no Moses. I'm a regular old child of God hiking through creation for a glimpse of the Master. Mind you, nature doesn't solve my problems, but it does reset my "worry-ometer." When I explore his wonders, I worry less. Care to join me? You don't need a degree in science or a month in the rain forest to find wonder. All you need is a willing heart and a few minutes of time to intentionally see, slow, and connect with God and creation. This book will show you how.

How to Use This Book

These chapters are intended to be savored, read leisurely at your own pace. Dive into wonder with whatever chapter catches your fancy. For the sake of organization, the book is divided into five sections based on habitat: Gifts of the Field, Gifts of the Air, Gifts of the Deep, Gifts of the Mountains and Gifts of the Desert. Bear in mind, however, that the creatures have not read the book and may also crawl, swim or fly in other locations.

In each chapter you will meet an ordinary object of nature. When we peer within the ordinary, details of extraordinary wonder are revealed and provide a peg on which to hang hope:

- Discover the locking mechanism within a feather and find the secret to spiritual strength.
- Peel back the layers of a leaf to learn the art of prayer.
- Explore the wing of a butterfly. See how the scale reflects light, much as God's light is reflected in our own lives.

At the close of each chapter, I encourage you to experience each wonder firsthand through an activity I call a "Wondercise." Essential items for each Wondercise are a notebook and a pen or pencil. Any additional materials necessary for each activity will be listed under "Knapsack Needs." Sometimes the activity is simply a contemplative walk. Other times the activity will involve a nitty-gritty, sensory experience—investigating a sprouted seed, tugging on ragged tree bark, or getting tactile with a dead fish (come on, lose the attitude, you do this all the time when you cook a salmon fillet). Sometimes the activity may seem a bit childish. So what? Give yourself permission to play. After all, Jesus challenged each one of us to become like a child. A child is wonder-full.

These simple, hands-on explorations in nature can stimulate your powers of observation and restore your sense of wonder and awe in the Creator and his creation. Each chapter concludes with an encouraging "Promise of Hope" from scripture. As you participate in these activities, you become a co-author with me in this unwrapping of wonder. I would love to hear about your journey into wonder—just visit my website at www.thedivinenatureproject.com and share your experiences.

Just so you know, reading this book will not make you an expert on nature. This book is not a field guide to identify what we see as much as it is a field guide to God—helping us to become better acquainted with the Creator through his creation. Nature is complex. I don't intend to answer the endless mysteries it holds. I couldn't. This is not a science textbook. Nor is it a treatise on evolution. Other writers examine those topics in great detail. The purpose of this book is to inspire wonder and appreciation for the works of art God has made. May you be drawn closer to the Craftsman's side, fret less about daily living and fall deeper in love with the one who made it all.

So come. Prepare to enter his presence in creation. Nature is a gift. And when we unwrap the gift, we will discover more of nature, God, and ourselves one wonder at a time. It's time to open the box.

PART I
Gifts of the Field

"God's gifts put man's best dreams to shame."
–Elizabeth Barrett Browning

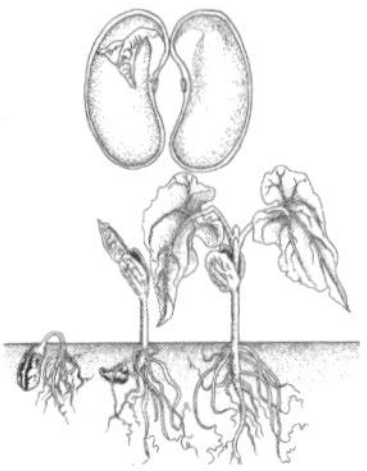

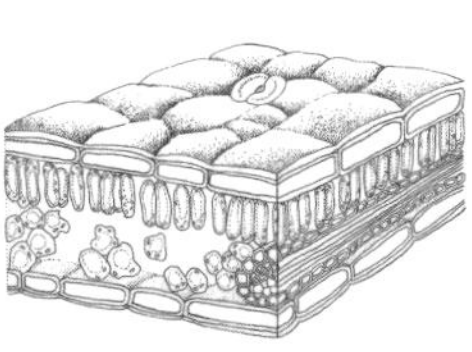
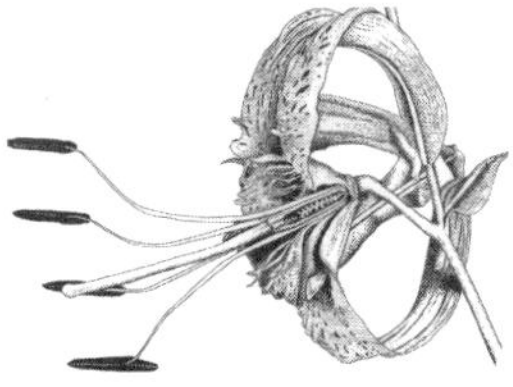

1

Grace Sings on Cricket Wings

"I do not at all understand the mystery of grace—only that it meets us where we are but does not leave us where it found us."
-Anne Lamott

Normal kids have a dog, cat, or perhaps a fish for a pet. I was not normal. My pet had an exoskeleton. My pet wore its ears on its knees. And my pet lived in a bamboo pagoda. At least his name was normal. Cricket was a cricket.

Bought on the streets of Chinatown in Los Angeles circa 1970, I carried him home to the suburbs of Orange County where he spent long nights calling to the crickets just beyond the screen of my bedroom window. I can still remember lying in bed, transfixed by his pure and simple song. Many a summer night of my childhood, the unmerited favor of the cricket song lulled me to sleep.

Crickets have captivated our species with their song for two-thousand years. Cricket keeping began in the Tang Dynasty (618-906 A.D.) as a pastime of aristocrats and emperor's concubines. Eventually the cricket-collecting custom spread to the common peoples of China and became an honored Chinese tradition.

Yet crickets are not the only singing insects. Lang Elliot, author of *The Song of Insects*[1], reveals four basic families of insect musicians: crickets, katydids, grasshoppers, and cicadas. Within each family are specialized groups. Consider the conehead katydids (I am not making this up; there are twenty-two species of coneheads of the katydid kind in North America). Their unique tune consists of a raspy sort of buzzing song. Contrast this with the slant-faced grasshoppers (again, I speak the truth) who are known for their more subtle, soft, and muffled song. I cite these differences to share with you that the rich sound of summer's orchestra consists of many insect musicians, each playing its own instrument. My favorite continues to be the cricket, as he occupies a nostalgic corner of my heart.

While I spent hours watching my fenced fiddler perform, effortlessly rubbing his wings together, it wasn't till years later in a college entomology class that I actually learned how the cricket produces its characteristic chirp. Remember the childhood trick of playing the comb with your fingernail? The process is quite similar. Each wing of a male cricket is designed with a large, toothed, ridge-like vein underneath, topped with a file-like scraper. Raising his wings at a forty-five degree angle, he prepares to perform, drawing the ridge-like teeth (think comb) beneath one wing against the scraper (think nail) on the upper edge of the other wing. Female crickets lack these defined, sound-producing structures on their wings. They do, however, have ears to hear. Ingeniously tucked just below their kneecaps, these ears (small oval discs, much like the eye of a needle) allow them to tune in to their suitors' songs. How cool is that?

Following the cricket-collecting stage of my adolescence, I eventually emerged into the safe and sound stage of adulthood. Much as my cricket in the cage, I sang the song of sameness. Ordinary days follow predictable nights. Life was good but routine. For seventeen years, my husband and I pastored a church. Much of my identity was tied to that church. I had become the classic PW (pronounced "P-Dub," that great moniker bestowed on all pastor's wives)—a good wife, multi-tasking mother, and weekly Bible study leader. My life consisted of a heavy dose of church with a touch of my passion—field biology—sprinkled on the side. I kept these spheres neatly divided, separated by my erroneous belief that church and biology didn't mix.

During those years I kept God much as I kept my pet cricket—caged, and safely ensconced in my routine, my demands, and my comfort zone. He performed on my schedule; his song was solely for my enjoyment. I saw to it that I fed my God regularly with church attendance and all things religious. I tossed him tasty morsels of deeds done in his name. I liked my God in the cage. This way, I controlled my life. Were I to free him from the cage, I risked a life turned upside down, changed and unknown.

My life became fenced within my fears. My comfort zone defined a happy little enclosure all about me. I was secure. Secure in my relationships. Secure in my job. Secure in my church. Security and sameness swallowed my soul. My life resembled a walnut, neatly compartmentalized and tucked in a smooth, round shell. And God, being God, let me have my way for a time. But he was about to teach me a lesson, in a shell-breaking,

"SINGING" SPRING FIELD CRICKET (Gryllus veletis)

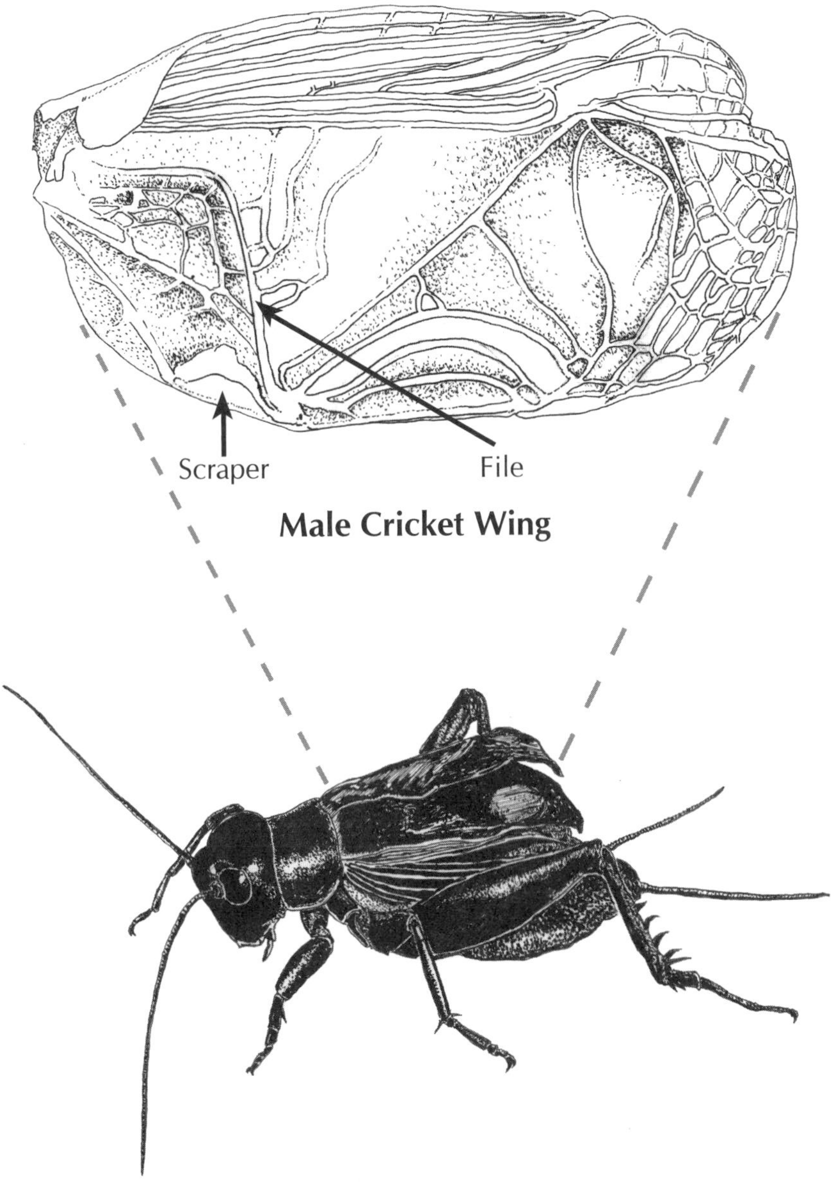

cage-busting, unscheduled, and very non-routine way.

Before we go there, it is crucial to know what happened to my caged cricket. Eventually, after days of feeding Cricket lettuce, bran and watermelon slices, a delectable feast to be sure, I began to wrestle with reason. On the one hand, I enjoyed my pet dutifully serenading me to sleep each night. On the other, it pained me to see him caged in an artificial life of sameness. Although he voraciously chomped on melon, much of the day he lay listless. My conscience gnawed at my mind. The thought that Cricket may die in his bamboo prison terrified me.

One night, as the crickets in the distance called to him, I pushed the screen off my window and released Cricket into his element, free to be. I imagined him scurrying over the fresh garden soil, his legs brushing against the carrot tops as he raced to his kind. With the chorus of crickets drumming in my ears, I knew I heard Cricket singing his pure and clear song of freedom.

It would be thirty years before I would hear that grace-filled song again. And when I did, it came not on cricket wings, but on the wings of God.... In 2006, my husband received three unsolicited job offers in a period of nine months. A sense of impending doom hung heavy on my heart as I saw change hovering just above the horizon. Confronted with three of my deepest fears—change, risk, and the unknown—I entered a phase of resistance. I did not want to move. Period. My resistance prevailed, and my husband politely refused the first two offers. However, as often is the case when God has a plan, the third job offer appeared. Worn down by God's persistence, I acquiesced and my husband accepted the challenge to revive a struggling, dying church in a rural community. This job, incidentally, made the first two job offers look like a day at the beach. With the faith of a flea, I struggled to grasp any thread of hope to carry me through. I knew in my heart that God had my back, but my brain strained to catch up with my heart.

During this year of turmoil, I learned to listen to the Master. Little did I know he was preparing to give me a new song. What needed to happen was a blending of tones, a symphonic merger, if you will.

Like that fiddler cricket making beautiful music with two structurally different wings, I needed to unite the wing of my biologist "bow" with the "string" of my Christianity. United wings are harmonic wings. Just one problem: I was out of practice. No, that's not entirely true. I had never practiced. I kept my "wings" in pristine condition, silent and separate.

Catholic priest and author Thomas Berry eloquently explained the mechanics of merging nature with spirituality:

> The outer world is necessary for the inner world; they are not two worlds, but a single world with two aspects.... We need the sun, the moon, the stars, the rivers and the mountains and birds, the fish in the sea, to evoke a world of mystery, to evoke the sacred. It gives us a sense of awe.[2]

I believed this. I knew firsthand the benefits of uniting the outer world of nature with the inner world of the soul. Yet I remained silent on sharing the power of God in nature. Perhaps I needed rosin, the human fiddler's friend. Let me explain. Rosin, a natural component of tree sap, allows the bow to grip the strings of the instrument and is responsible for producing full resonating sound. No rosin? Then no grip, no sound. I needed spiritual rosin to allow my "string"and "bow" to resonate with a new, beautiful song that sang of the wonders of creation.

The move to central Oregon only magnified my need to refine my purpose. I left behind my job and close friends. I wrestled with purpose for months. Then on a crisp fall day in 2007, I hiked to a knoll overlooking the Big Deschutes River. Leaning back against an ancient, gnarled Ponderosa pine I prayed,

> Okay God, here I am. Show me how to unite the spheres of my life. Give me purpose. Help me glorify you with my passion for creation.

And my faithful Father answered his lost and lonely child. Deep in my soul I received refreshing raindrops of grace—the rosin I needed.

The Greek word for grace is *charis*, which literally means "that which affords joy, pleasure, delight, sweetness, charm, loveliness." With great pleasure, and much joy, I finally felt free to pursue the person God created me to be—the wildlife loving, wilderness wandering me—instead of who I thought I was expected to be. This didn't happen overnight. And it certainly wasn't easy. Slowly, one small step at a time, God led me forward on this journey.

God infuses the symphony of our lives with grace notes: we have the freedom to choose the melody that makes our lives sing. We are not to play a life score written by someone else. We are free to dance to the beat of our own heart, guided by the conductor of life himself.

WONDERCISE

Nature's Thermometer

In 1897, American physicist and inventor Amos Dolbear discovered how to calculate air temperature in Fahrenheit using the rate of a cricket's chirp.[3] You can too, using his formula.

Knapsack Needs:

- Thermometer
- Ears to hear

On a warm summer's night (over 55° F), grab a lawn chair, go outside, and enjoy nature's symphony. Impress your friends and neighbors by estimating the air temperature counting cricket chirps. A cricket chirps faster as temperatures rise and slower when temperatures fall. Dust off your math brain and try this nifty experiment. I sense your tension at the mention of the word math. Relax, it's not that hard. Using an equation is no different from following a recipe. Just plug in the ingredients and stir the numbers:

$$50 + \frac{N - 40}{4} = T$$

N is the number of chirps in 1 minute, and T is for temperature.

Math challenged? You can also use the following equation (modified from Dolbear's original), though it may give a slightly less accurate estimate:

$$40 + N = T$$

N is the number of chirps in 15 seconds, and T is for temperature.

In plain English, this means you count the number of chirps in 15 seconds and add 40 to this number. This gives an estimate of the temperature in degrees Fahrenheit.

EXAMPLE:

1. Count the number of cricket chirps you hear in 15 seconds (for illustration, let's imagine we count 22 chirps in 15 seconds.)
2. Add 40 to this number: 22 + 40 = 62
3. The estimated temperature, then, is 62 degrees.

Just for fun, grab a real thermometer and check the accuracy of your "cricket thermometer." Oh, and don't forget to enjoy the song in the midst of the math.

Promise of Hope

"Here's what I want you to do: Find a quiet, secluded place so you won't be tempted to role play before God. Just be there as simply and honestly as you can imagine. The focus will shift from you to God, and you will begin to sense his Grace" (Matthew 6:6, *The Message*).

2

SEED, GLORIOUS SEED

"I have come that they may have life, and have it to the full."
John 10:10

Life with a biologist for a mother is never dull. Consider the day I helped my then ten-year-old son Michael connect the dots between an orange and its seed. As he painstakingly struggled to remove each seed from the orange he was about to consume, he innocently wondered out loud where seeds come from and why oranges had to have seeds. Warning—don't ever ask a biologist "why" without expecting an in-depth explanation. I shared with Michael the literal definition of a fruit—the ripened ovary of a seed plant. Bad idea. The word ovary shuttered snack time and ended conversation. Michael's taste for fruit soured for a solid week before his love of food triumphed and he was able to move beyond Webster's definition. Sometimes ignorance is bliss. Who knew?

What you are about to read may upset your apple cart of beliefs about fruits and vegetables. For instance, if your idea of a fruit salad is a bowl of bananas, oranges and grapes—think again. Cucumbers, tomatoes and olives? Fruit salad. Peas, beans and peanuts? More fruit. If it has a seed, it's a fruit. Any part of a plant without seeds—cabbage, broccoli, spinach and so on—falls into the vegetable bin.

Fruits are plentiful. Adam Gollner, in *The Fruit Hunters,* estimates there are 240,000 to 500,000 different plant species that bear fruit[1]. And these fruits, often sweet and showy, get the attention. Whether you want to call that orange an ovary or not is a personal choice, but the fact remains that a fruit is a seed "purse" of sorts, for it carries valuable currency of the plant—the golden coins of its genetic code. Yet the seed, or embryo, is often swallowed up in the fame and fanfare of fruit. And we miss the miracle of the seed.

One who did not miss the miracle of the seed was Henry David

GERMINATION OF A BEAN SEED

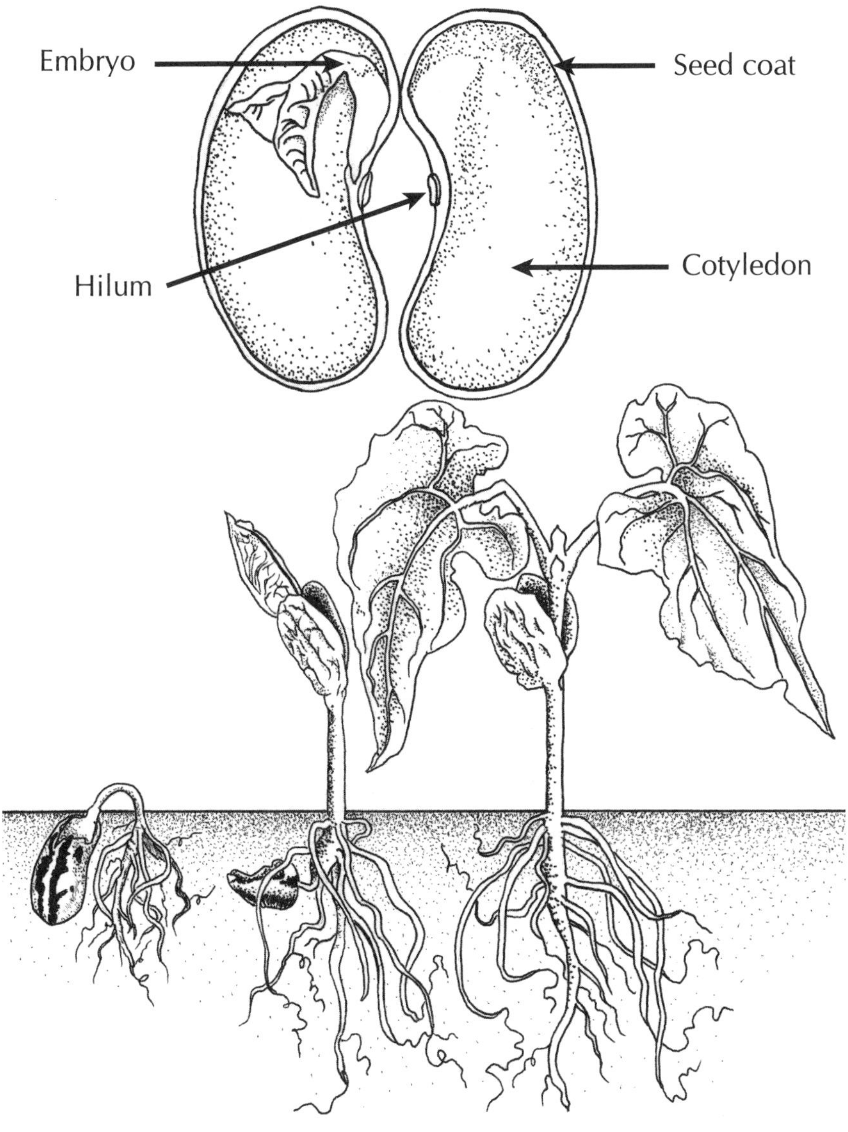

Thoreau, widely recognized for his literary masterpiece, *Walden*. Yet Thoreau spent years dedicated to the study of seeds. His last and lesser known manuscript, *Faith in a Seed*, is a work on the miracle of seeds. Says Thoreau: "I have great faith in a seed. Convince me that you have a seed there, and I am prepared to expect wonders."[2] Let's crack open the wonder of the seed.

Seeds come in a dazzling array of shapes and sizes. Consider the world's largest seed, the *Coco-de-mer*, also known as "the double coconut." This unusual seed from the fan palm, *Lodoicea maldivica*, can grow to twelve inches in length and weigh up to sixty-six pounds. At the opposite end of the spectrum are orchids, which produce the world's smallest known seeds. One orchid fruit alone can hold up to four million, dust-particle-like seeds (Having spent time as a seed-counting, number-crunching biologist, I tip my hat to the very patient biologist who discovered that minuscule fact).

No matter their size, all seeds have one thing in common: life. Seeds deliver the goods. They transfer the genetic material to the next generation. A single seed, which no scientist has ever been able to manufacture, contains everything it needs for life and lies nestled under the covers of its protective seed coat.

That seed—an inanimate, hard packet of life—sleeps. Until germination. Germination is the process of waking the tiny embryo of the seed, arousing it from the slumber of its hibernation to reach its full potential. If not for germination, the seed would remain forever stunted in its dormant state.

Several things are necessary for germination. To awaken a seed, water, oxygen and proper temperature are required. Given the proper conditions, the seed will absorb water and swell, thereby breaking out of its protective seed coat. Sometimes water alone is not enough to penetrate the coat, and an additional process called scarification is required. *Scarify* is what it sounds like—to cut or soften the wall of the resistant seed coat—and derives from the Latin, "to scratch open."

If you are a gardener, you may have committed the act of scarification—but don't be alarmed! Have you ever soaked beans or pea seeds overnight before planting? That's scarification. Have you used a file or sandpaper to nick the seed coat of a bean or lupine? That's scarification. Sometimes the tough seed needs roughing up to encourage germination.

And sometimes in life, we need the Lord to come along and scarify our stubborn seed coats of fear or doubt to move us to our potential. Consider the life of Gregor Mendel, Austrian scientist, monk and prolific gardener who became known as the founder of genetic science. Mendel's path to priesthood and his understanding of peas was described as "tortuous" by author Robin Henig in *The Monk in the Garden*. When Mendel did achieve success, it came "not because of something he had set out to do, but almost in spite of it."[3] Can I relate to that! Often times, God has curious ways of easing us into our purposes, sometimes gently, sometimes not—until we reach the potential he has gifted us with. His ways are best. "As the heavens are higher than the earth, so are my ways higher than your ways and my thoughts than your thoughts" (Isaiah 55:9).

Mendel's journey from poverty to pea notoriety took nearly a century. And it was a circuitous route. Born, as Johann Mendel, into a poor farming family in 1822, he soon outgrew his farming roots. Henig describes Mendel as a young man feeling destined for a different way of life. It seems his ticket to leave the farm first came in educational opportunities and later in the religious relief of a monastery. In 1843 Johann Mendel joined the Augustinian Abbey and became Gregor Mendel.

For years, Mendel's life consisted of following an agenda written by others. His father envisioned him a farmer and considered him a colossal failure when he left to pursue education. When he entered the monastery, the priests groomed him for the position of parish priest to attend to the needs of the sick and dying. But Mendel buckled under the emotional strain and spent weeks in bed, suffering both physically and spiritually. Next came teacher training; yet, due to extreme test anxiety, he failed the examination for certification—twice. Talk about an identity crisis! By the providence of God, one of Mendel's examiners recognized his talent and stated that "if he is given opportunity for more exhaustive study together with access to better sources of information he will soon be able to fit himself."[4] Soon Mendel began studies at the Royal Imperial University of Vienna. And "fit himself" he did. Freed from the demands of others, he explored the worlds of botany, mathematics, and natural sciences which prepared him for the famous garden discoveries and experiments to come.

Upon completion of his university studies, Mendel returned to the monastery. Perhaps as a respite from the nineteenth century version of "purpose driven life" stress, Mendel found his way to the garden where he was at home among the vines. Intrigued by seeds and their offspring, he threw himself into research. There, in the glass house where he had gained gardening rights, Mendel devoted six long years to the study of peas. Mendel would select certain plants for specific "character traits," such as seed shape, color, blossom location, or even plant height. He then painstakingly hand pollinated each plant with a pair of tweezers and a camel hair paintbrush. Mendel witnessed the germination and growth of some twenty-eight thousand pea plants, kept meticulous records, and documented the results of these hybrid crosses. Henig estimates that Mendel "must have counted a total of more than 10,000 pea plants, 40,000 blossoms, and a staggering 300,000 peas."[5] From these planned pea pregnancies Mendel was able to predict the outcome of appearance in the next generation. In 1866, Mendel published his remarkable findings in an article called "Experiments on Plant Hybridization" in the *Proceedings of the Nature Research Society of Brunn.*

The response? Virtually none. Recognition? Didn't happen. No one found the results to have significant meaning. Mendel's scientific genius went unnoticed. Yet Mendel seemed undaunted and often chanted the phrase "Meine Zeit wird schon kommen"—"My time will come."[6]

In 1884 Mendel died in obscurity. Yet nearly thirty years after Mendel first played matchmaker among the peas, his ideas surfaced again. The year was 1900. This time the world was ready. Three scientists working independently on problems of heredity unknowingly reproduced the research and results Mendel completed three decades earlier. Eventually Mendel was credited as the author of the "laws of heredity" and became known as the father of genetics. Mendel's time had come.

God's timing is not our timing. Often our schedule does not jive with God's schedule. During the delay, he is building patience and humility into our lives. What we often count as failure, God counts as preparation, training for the next task he has in store.

> And we know that in all things, God works for the good of those who love him, who have been called according to his purpose (Romans 8:28).

Life has no wasted experiences. Each difficult and uncomfortable experience of Mendel's life served to bring him to his full potential. Through his "failures," Mendel transitioned from brokenness to abundance. He lived the abundant life—in spite of himself.

Often times, in order for us to blossom into the abundant life God has in store for us, we must accept our own spiritual brokenness—just as germination requires the seed coat to be broken. We must be willing to allow God to shape us, pierce us, and even divert us from the path we have so carefully charted out so that he can transform us from dormancy to maturity. God longs for us to burst through the walls of fear and doubt so that he can take us to life's next level en route to the grand and fruitful stage he envisions for each of us.

Have you settled into dormancy? Are you lacking the life-giving water necessary to initiate the germination process? Do you long for an abundant, seed-coat-busting life? Abandon your dry and routine life to him. Risk heat. Risk exposure. Risk growth. And take heart. Jesus tells us,

> Unless a kernel of wheat falls to the ground and dies, it remains only a single seed. But if it dies, it produces many seeds (John 12:24).

Tucked at the core of our very being, lies the seed to an abundant life, neatly packaged and awaiting germination. We need only to drink deeply from the fount of living water. The water is available. The water is free. And the water can empower us to burst out of our spiritual seed coats.

Allow God to unleash his power in your life. Dream big. Grow great. Sprout where you are planted. And live. Abundantly.

WONDERCISE

Seed Play

Explore the world of the seed and its germination. Discover special "seed features" God created to ensure its survival and abundance.

Knapsack Needs:

- Bean seeds
- Random packets of seeds
- Hand lens
- Container of water

Observe the bean seed with your hand lens. On the concave side of the bean notice the small white bump, or scar, called the hilum. This scar marks the point of attachment of the bean to the ovary wall—the umbilical cord, if you will. Turn the seed over in your hand. How does it feel? Is it soft or hard to the touch? Smooth or rough? You are discovering the seed's protective "coat," aptly named as it guards the seed from the hazards of drought, extreme heat, or other conditions not ideal for germination. In this state, a seed is dormant.

Open the packets of seed and pour a few into separate piles. Study the seed coats of several varieties. Each seed has a unique coat: a bean has a very different appearance than that of a beet seed. Feel the difference.

AWAKEN THE SEED

Soak the bean seed in water for twenty-four hours. Observe the seed with a hand lens. You will notice the seed has swelled. Using a sharp knife or fingernail, gently pry the seed open. It will separate into two halves, called cotyledons, the food storage organs. Look closely for the miniature bean plant, or embryo. Notice the tiny undeveloped leaves and the rudimentary stem. Imagine the root which will develop from the base of the stem. There before your eyes, neatly packaged within the bean, lies the entire future of the plant.

SEEDS IN NATURE

Step outside. Survey the flowers and shrubs in your yard, neighborhood, or nursery for evidence of seeds. Seeds display differently depending upon the plant. For example, the dandelion seed heads form balls of fluff, with the individual seeds tethered within. The seeds of the California Poppy, on the other hand, are concealed in saber shaped pods, which will twist open upon drying and scatter seeds about. Once scattered, these seeds will rest in dormancy until the cycle of growth begins again.

Use your seed "field trip" to search for three different types of seeds. Describe your observations of each seed, including how they are the same and how they are different, in your notebook. Thank God for the diversity of seeds and the potential life each one holds.

Promise of Hope

"His divine power has given us everything we need for life and godliness through our knowledge of him who called us by his own glory and goodness" (2 Peter 1:3).

3
FLOWER POWER

"I do not think I have ever seen anything more beautiful than the bluebell I have been looking at. I know the beauty of our Lord by it."
–Gerard Manley Hopkins

Beauty in a bluebell. Hopkins knew how to read God's book of nature. I did not. In 1986, I was so busy collecting and cataloging flowers, I skipped beauty in the name of botany. Scouring the slopes of the steep and scenic Mill Creek Canyon, armed with my plant press, collecting vials, and portable microscope, nothing could deter me from my mission: to document the flora of Mill Creek Canyon. And I did—bluebells included. Two hundred forty-two plant specimens, one rattlesnake, and countless ticks later, I completed my master's thesis. Each floral "trophy" was pressed and mounted, securely lodged in an herbarium for perpetuity.

But did I know "the beauty of our Lord by it" as Gerard Manley Hopkins so eloquently stated? Hardly. Perfect praise was consumed in a collection haze. Reminds me of how some view the weekly worship experience—collecting church attendance much as I collected flowers. Rush in, shake a few hands, press into the pews of the "church-arium," then hurry out the doors and return to life as normal. Admittedly, some weeks I miss worship. Oh, I'm in the building—physically—but did I gaze on the wonder of his holiness? Seek his face? Praise his grace? Did I fall to my knees and say, "Thou art worthy, O Lord, to receive glory and honor and power: for thou hast created all things, and for thy pleasure they are and were created" (Revelation 4:11, KJV).

Flowers are one of those miracles God created for our pleasure. As Hopkins stated, a flower can reveal to us the beauty of our Lord. But flowers also exist for the re-creation of their own species. In their handbook of flowers, authors Scoble and Field write, "Flowers are beautiful and fragrant for a reason: to spread pollen and engender their kind."[1] Flowers and their powers are a wonder. Let's poke our noses into a flower for a deeper appreciation of God's botanical creations—and discover how lilies can lead us to worship.

When he created the flower he thought form and function. Sketch the lily in your mind's eye.

Envision the petals stretching outward, revealing the reproductive powers which dance before you in the form of the female pistil and the male stamen (Figure 1). The pistil erupts like a fountain from the flower and is composed of stigma, style and ovary (think egg) while the male stamen is a stalk-like filament bearing the anther (think pollen)—yet because the flower is a stationary object, never the twain shall meet. Pollination is God's way of bringing the two together via insects, birds and in some cases on the wings of the wind. Does the meaning behind the phrase "the birds and the bees" make sense now? That scent of desire—the fragrance emitted by the flower—serves to draw a pollinator into its midst to join the pollen with the pistil. Which brings me to the heart of worship.

Just as a flower is designed to draw the pollinator into its center for the purpose of re-creation, worship is meant to escort us into the very heart of God for our own spiritual re-creation. Worship is why we were created. And worship feeds our souls. I crave the sweet, nourishing nectar of worship. I long to quench my thirst with his grace, to hover on the breath of his mercy as he welcomes me into his presence. I long to engage my senses with the loveliness of him. I want worship. Deep, pure and holy worship.

Yet, in all honesty, I struggle. Struggle to grasp that life-sustaining connection that worship offers. Some days I am stuck in the shallows of "surface church" and pure worship eludes me. It's been said that beauty is in the eye of the beholder. And the beauty of worship can get lost in the "I" of the beholder.

As a pastor's wife for more years than I care to admit, I have squandered worship trying to ignore prying eyes. I feel the stares boring into me. I focus inward on me, myself and I, instead of turning my gaze heavenward towards God. If you think I imagine I'm being watched, I have proof in a bevy of comments people have shared after the service. Consider some winners to remember—or forget (oh, how I wish I could):

"I watched that spider drop onto your head and walk around your hair like it was his web." (This woman was so stricken by the accosting spider that she interrupted the service to notify my husband who promptly

BASIC FLOWER STRUCTURE

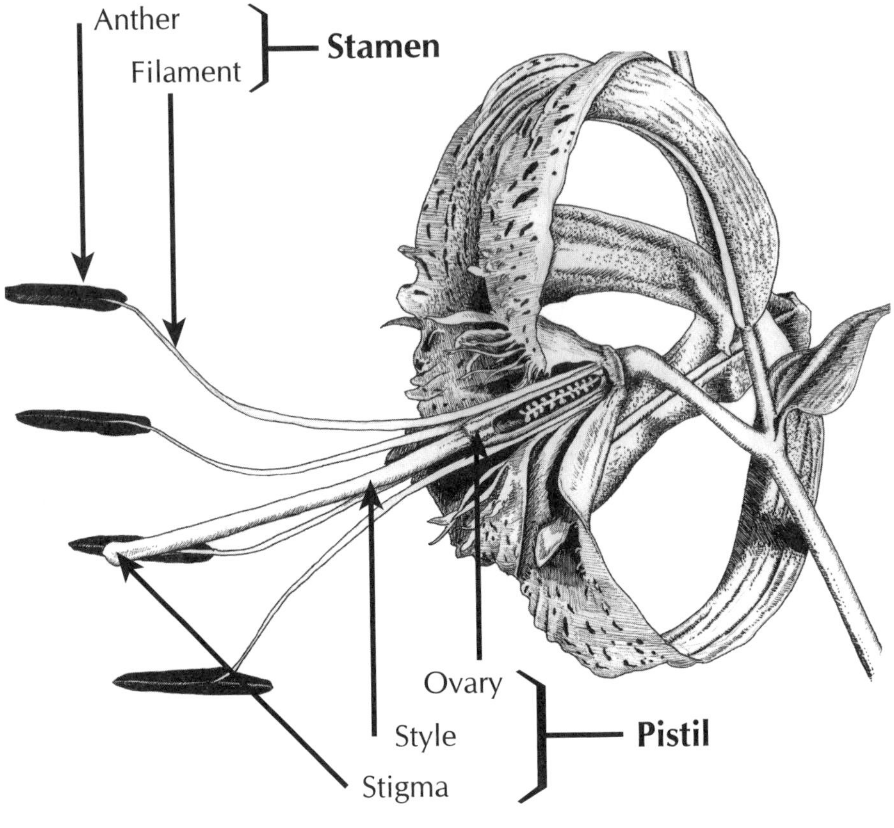

Lily

plucked the arachnid from my locks—an incident that was beyond embarrassing.)

And speaking of hair, consider this gem:

"Oh, my gosh. What happened to your hair? Who cut it and, oh my gosh, what a terrible cut! I just feel so bad for you."

But enough about beauty. Comments also fall into what I call the misjudged and misunderstood category:

"Did you and the pastor have a fight? I noticed you weren't sitting together today."

"When I saw you sitting next to the pastor, I was just amazed. I thought the worship leader was his wife. I didn't expect *you* to be his wife."

I could go on, but lest you think me to be the annoyed, unhappy wife of a pastor, I'm not. Okay, so I am a little annoyed but not unhappy. I get it; the position of a pastor and his wife is a public one. And while I love to lift our voices together in praise, I also long for privacy to lift my heart to the God of the universe in worship. Holy worship—pure and personal worship. So whether I allow worship to be derailed by idle chatter, or by idol clatter, the point is, worship is about God, not about us.

One thing that helps me come to worship better prepared is to check my ego at the door. I need to come down from on high and perform an altitude adjustment. That's right, *altitude*.

After all, the primary Hebrew word for worship is *Shachah*, which means

> to prostrate (in homage to royalty or God): bow (self) down, crouch, fall down (flat), humbly beseech … do reverence, make to stoop, worship.[2]

Or consider the Greek word for worship, *Proskuneo*, which means

> to kiss, like a dog licking his master's hand, to fawn or crouch to, pay homage to.

And in English, it literally means to ascribe worth to something.

So why can't we just call it *worthship*? After all, he is worthy, more than worthy. So here's my definition:

Worthship: to draw near to God and give him praise; to fall on our face in reverence and humbly come before him; stillness in the beauty of his holiness.

For a brief moment in this hectic life, worship allows us to be drawn out of ourselves and next to his side, into his presence. Worship allows us to forget our cares and ourselves and catch a glimpse of his glory. When we dwell there, in that timeless state, our weary souls are restored.

Which brings me back to flowers. Throughout history, humans have used flowers to express their sentiments, commemorate important rituals, and beautify their surroundings. Flowers, too, are good for the soul. With more than 270,000 species of flowers known to exist it comes as no surprise that flowers play an important role in our lives. Food, romance, and even medicine can be derived from flowers. Flowers can be therapeutic—literally.

Consider the story of the doctor who discovered both the medical and romantic value of the flower. Dr. William Withering was a physician with a botanical interest on the side, not at all unusual considering that for centuries humankind has depended on the medicinal value of plants. The practice of medicine could not exist without that knowledge. Many cures and treatments were intricately tied to the science of botany.

Author Jerry Norman tells the delightful story of how the flower played a role in Dr. Withering finding the love of his life. During 1768, one of Dr. Withering's patients was a young woman named Helena Cook, who ironically enjoyed painting flowers. To help with her convalescence, Dr. Withering would scour the countryside to gather new floral subjects for her to paint. "From all of this intense mutual study of flowers a budding romance blossomed and in 1772, Miss Cook married Dr. Withering."[3] Who says flowers aren't romantic?

But in addition to stirring romance in the heart, Dr. Withering discovered that flowers had the power to cure heart ailments. Specifically, a posy named foxglove—that old fashioned flower of fairy tales and English vales—had medicinal properties as a diuretic. The scientific name, *Digitalis purpurea*, means "finger-like" and is a reference to the shape of the flower, much like little gloves for the fingers (hence the additional name "folk's glove" a reference to gloves for fairies or small animals). Aside from the fairy tale nature of the flower, foxglove held some real world potential in the medical field.

Over a course of several years, Dr. Withering studied 158 patients treated with foxglove extract. One hundred and one of those patients found relief from congestive heart failure following prescribed dosages of the drug, called Digitalis, which is still used today as a treatment in heart disease.

Flowers can also treat the ailment of our hearts in wayward worship, when our minds have strayed and our hearts are heavy. Looking into the face of a flower can instill a sense of awe for the Creator who handcrafted such intricate, pure beauty. We would do well to consider the wise words of Ralph Waldo Emerson:

> Never lose an opportunity of seeing anything that is beautiful; for beauty is God's handwriting—a wayside sacrament. Welcome it in every fair face, in every fair sky, in every fair flower, and thank God for it as a cup of blessing.[4]

We need to give ourselves permission to stop along the busy highway called life. To stoop and smell the roses. To drink the cup of blessing offered in the beauty of a bluebell. And praise God above. For when we do, the aroma of praise ascends heavenward. That's worship.

WONDERCISE

Consider the Lilies of the Field

Make no mistake; God's creativity is evident when you begin to delve into the intricacies of flowers. See for yourself.

Knapsack Needs:

- Hand Lens
- A variety of fresh flowers, from your yard or a local flower stand

Spread the flowers out on a table. Examine each one. How do the flowers differ? Compare their size, shape, and color. Are they round or elongated, single or clustered? Does the number of petals differ with flower type? If so, how? Are the colors bold and vibrant, or modest and muted?

Don't be shy—look within the center of the flower. What parts are visible? Some flowers, like snapdragons and sweet peas, conceal their stamens and pistils. Using your hand lens, find the pistils and stamens and count the number of each. Do they differ in number? And last but not least, don't forget to inhale. Scented or not? If so, describe the scent.

Now venture outside and observe the diversity of flowers as they are found growing in nature. Contemplate the majesty of the master artist. Consider the hand of God in the wildflower's ability to germinate, grow, flower, and set seed in one short season with no maintenance needed. The cycle of wildflowers is one of his grandest creations.

And if God cares for the flowers, will he not care for you?

Promise of Hope

"See how the lilies of the field grow. They do not labor or spin. Yet I tell you that not even Solomon in all his splendor was dressed like one of these. If that is how God clothes the grass of the field...will he not much more clothe you, O you of little faith?" (Matthew 6:28-30).

4

THE LIVES of LEAVES

"True prayer is the engine of the world..."
–Pope Benedict XVI

Engines are powerhouses. Designed to convert energy into motion, engines get the job done. As a child, I loved (and I still love) Watty Piper's classic children's book, *The Little Engine that Could.* The story's hero is the small engine that triumphed in a task reserved for the bigger engines. That little engine summoned his strength, revved his engine to the refrain "I think I can, I think I can, I think I can," and summited the mountain.[1] Prayer, when done regularly and earnestly, elicits the effect of *The Little Engine That Could.* It gets us up and over the mountain we thought we could not climb.

Prayer is to our lives what leaves are to plants—a power source. Leaves are the food factories of the plant. Plants are unique in their ability to produce their own food through a process called photosynthesis (*photo* means "light," *syn* means "with," and *thesis* means "to make"). Using light, the leaf carbo-loads its daily energy needs.

Frankly, the very idea leaves me green with envy. Imagine if we as humans could synthesize our own dinner. No shopping, no food prep and no need to cook. We would be free to lie in the sun all day and soak up our nutritional needs. Overeating would be a thing of the past. Ah, well, but I digress.

The simplified version of food production in a leaf blade is this: The leaf captures light via little green cells, inhales a healthy supply of carbon dioxide, mixes in some water drawn up from the roots, and *shazam*! the leaf just manufactured sugar. In addition, the leaf serves up a dose of oxygen as a byproduct, which humans need for survival. And leaves perform this miracle every day.

The cross section of a leaf can be compared to a factory. When I

CROSS SECTION OF A LEAF

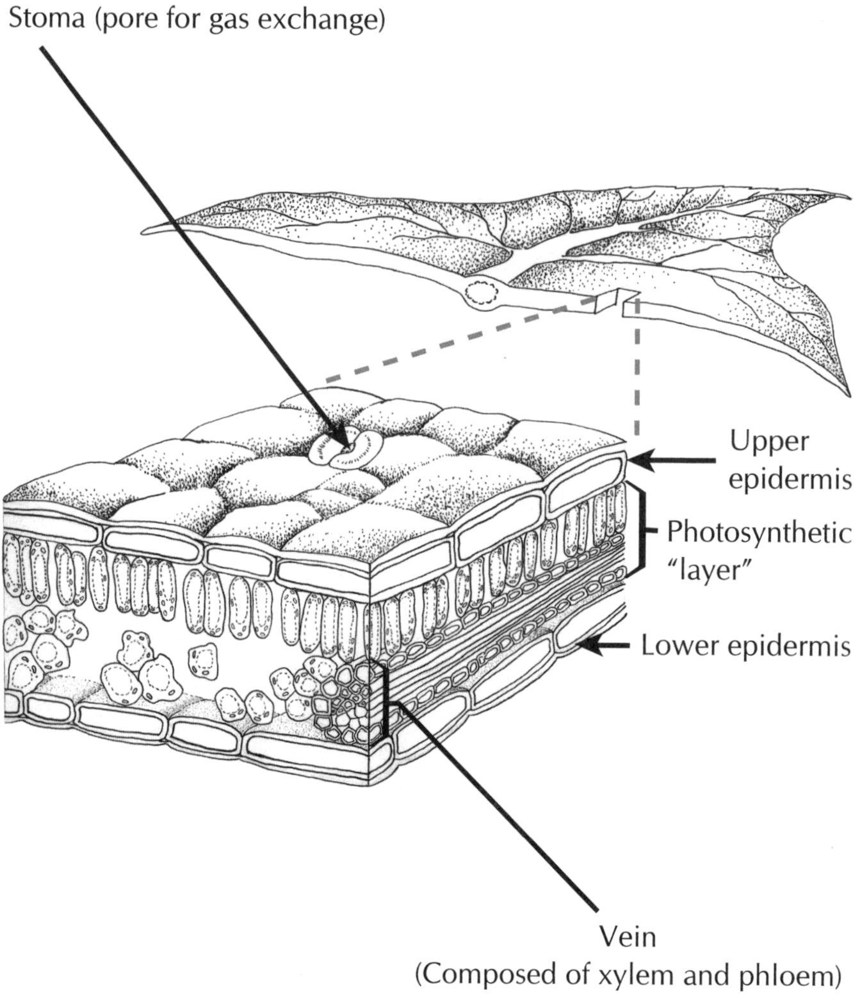

lived on the Oregon coast, one of my favorite things to do was to visit the Tillamook cheese factory. After a sampling of cheese, I explored the factory—visiting the floors to see how it operated. Today I invite you to join me on a leaf factory tour. Journey through an intricate arrangement of microscopic tubes and tunnels as we venture into the life of a leaf (and while carbohydrates are involved, I'm sorry to say there will be no free cheese samples on this tour).

One thin leaf sandwiches a three-story food factory of sorts, with each level housing a specific task-oriented department. On the top level, the leaf's "skin," or epidermis, protects the plant. The skin carefully regulates just who or what passes through the doors of the factory. Drop down to level two and enter the production line of the factory. Here the leaf works to capture the sunlight via "solar panels" (light-absorbing pigments). These panels harness light energy and transform it into rich carbohydrates, that usable form of energy necessary for the everyday growth of the plant. The bottom level is similar to the top and serves as the foundation of sorts, holding it all together.

Let's park on level two a moment. Sidled up to that conveyor belt spitting out the carbs, lies the crucial transport system for sap and all things fluid—the plant's circulatory system. The food that has been produced must now be moved throughout the plant using a detailed network of channels and tubes. Those veins of a leaf are the leaf's skeleton, the conduit through which the life source of the plant flows.

Oh, that prayer could flow through our lives as smoothly and freely as the transport of food and water in a plant's veins. Oh that we would faithfully fill our lives with prayer that ebbs with our praises, concerns, and cares and flows with the freshness of his sustaining love—an exchange of sorts, a smooth flowing system. Through the flow of prayer, we can trust that God has every detail of our lives under control. After all, details are his specialty.

God has orchestrated the details of cellular perfection where hundreds, if not thousands, of cells are working together to produce energy from the light source of the sun, manufacturing food, which is then transported to every cell of the plant.

In the same way that God provides the nourishment for plants, he provides spiritual nourishment for us. Prayer is the vehicle through which we can obtain the energy we need to carry on in the emotionally-draining world of life. Spiritual giant George Mueller said that after a time of reading the Word, he was moved to prayer, during which his "inner man almost invariably was nourished and strengthened."[2]

> So do not worry, saying, 'What shall we eat?' or 'What shall we drink?'... your heavenly father knows that you need them (Matthew 6:31-32).

Each day God is ready to provide all we need. He prepares the table and invites us to dine daily with him. We need only to arrive ready to be filled.

Being filled requires a certain level of emptiness. Again, within the confines of a leaf, this concept is illustrated perfectly. If we magnify the phloem tissue, whose job it is to transport the food, we find a cellular anomaly of sorts—a cell without a nucleus.

"What?" you may say. Or even, "So what?" Hang on, here is the so-what:

In each cell's delicate and fragile life, an organizational headquarters is needed. This job falls to the nucleus. Normally, each living cell contains a nucleus, the information and administration center, if you will. The nucleus is responsible for controlling cellular activity and houses the cell's genetic information. Because the nucleus is large and in charge and contains all the necessary information to keep the cell functioning, it consumes a considerable amount of cellular space. The nucleus alone occupies about ten percent of a cell's volume, making it one of the most prominent features of a cell. In most round and roly-poly cells, this does not present a problem.

However, in the streamlined, smooth, tubular plant cell, called a sieve tube, whose job it is to channel nutrients made in the leaf throughout the plant, having a chubby nucleus at its center would clog the flow of goods and present a problem. A very large and nucleated problem. Imagine trying to commute home in rush hour traffic. Wouldn't it be easier to drive if you were the only car on the road?

By virtue of a brilliant cellular design, plants avoid this problem. Their sieve cells are nucleus free. That's right. In plants, the nucleus in the sieve cell is mysteriously missing—normally a recipe for disaster and sure death. Not to worry, however, as each sieve cell is paired with a partner companion cell—a handy, lifesaving feature. This companion cell sits neatly attached to the sieve cell's hip, so to speak, and acts as the "brains" of the sieve cell. This tiny team of cells—a microscopic dynamic duo—work together to get the job done.

With the nucleus out of the way, the sieve cell now has every available millimeter of space in its cell to transport and move fluids. The efficiently-designed companion-sieve-cell team allows the plant to function in a more efficient manner. Freed from cellular clutter, fluids move unimpeded through the plant.

Which brings me back to the importance of emptiness. God longs to unleash the flow of his Spirit through our lives. In order to be filled, however, we must be empty. We must lose the nucleus of worry, so his power can flow through us unobstructed. The challenge is to become an empty vessel.

After all, emptiness begs to be filled. Consider the widow of 2 Kings chapter 4, a woman well acquainted with emptiness. Her husband had died and creditors were on the way to collect her two sons as slaves. Even her pantry was nearly empty. All she had was a little oil. Scripture says she "cried out to Elisha." No wonder. While Elisha was willing to help her, his technique seems odd to me. He sent her to gather more emptiness. "Go around and ask all your neighbors for empty jars." Now I could understand if he told her to borrow oil, olives, even a shekel or two; but empty jars?

She must have thought he was crazy. *Empty jars? What good will those do me?* Yet she obeyed. She sent her sons to collect the jars, and God supplied the oil until not an empty jar was left. This story illustrates that it is precisely when we are empty that God can work best in us. Empty vessels long to be filled—to overflowing levels.

We would do well to empty ourselves—for when we are empty, then God can fill us with his fullness.

> Ask and it will be given to you … for everyone who asks receives… (Matthew 7:7).

Prayer unleashes power. Why, then, do we skip prayer? I believe it is because we are full. Full of ourselves, our ways, and our will. We need a regular catharsis.

Often times, in the daily swirl of life, I need a time out. Time to empty myself of life's little burdens I have picked up along the way. Time to heed the words of Jesus:

> Come to me, all you who are weary and burdened and I will give you rest (Matthew 11:28).

Taking time for a cup of tea, I find this rest with a few leaves, a pot of water, and a whisper of prayer.

The story of tea's humble origin is found in a popular Chinese legend. It all began rather serendipitously. In approximately 2700 B.C. China's Emperor Shen Nong, demanded that his subjects boil his water for sanitary health reasons. One day, the wind blew a few leaves into his water, imparting a delightful aroma to the brew, which the emperor sampled. He found the drink refreshing and rejuvenating. Thus, the tradition of tea leaves gave rise to centuries of tea time, which I enjoy to this day.

My afternoon cup of comfort finds me in good company. The habit of English afternoon tea was said to have originated with Anna Maria Stanhope, the seventh Duchess of Bedford, who suffered from "that sinking feeling" during the late afternoon.[3] Customary of her day, people subsisted on two meals a day: in the morning and again at eight o'clock at night. The afternoon pot of tea and light snack was Stanhope's way to tide herself over and boost energy levels. The tea time tradition took hold.

Are you tired and weary? Do you need to rest? How about a cup of tea for your soul? Sit down. Pour hot water over a few leaves. Hold out your soul's empty cup. And prepare to be filled as you sip and worship.

WONDERCISE

Appreciating Leaves

In this activity you will discover the variety of leaves and realize their importance in our lives.

Knapsack Needs:

- Paper bag
- Hand lens
- Clear plastic bag
- Twist tie
- Supplies to brew a cup of tea

LEAF WATCH

Enjoy a walk in your neighborhood. Observe the diversity of leaves on flowers, trees and shrubs. Notice the differences in shape, size, and texture (hairy or smooth, thick or thin). Collect a few leaves in your paper bag to study over a cup of tea. Sketch your observations in your notebook.

Choose one leaf to hold between your fingertips. Contemplate the wonder tucked in between the upper and lower surfaces of this leaf. Think of the hundreds of cells contained inside and the intricate details of the job they do to keep the plant alive. Remember the companion cell working side by side with the sieve cell in a detailed and perfectly choreographed way? If that is how God cares for the leaf of a plant, will he not care for you? Lift your praise and prayers to God. He is faithful.

EXTRA-ORDINARY WONDER

Witness the wonder of photosynthesis. Place a clear plastic bag around a plant stem containing a few leaves. Secure tightly with a twist tie. Leave on for twenty-four hours. The next day observe the bag. What has changed? The evidence of photosynthesis will be present in the form of condensation. While you went about your daily life, the leaf was busy producing the food it needed and releasing oxygen and water into the environment. Every day, all around us, leaves make a difference—in their lives and ours. Thank God.

Promise of Hope

"Do not be anxious about anything, but in everything, by prayer and petition, with thanksgiving, present your requests to God. And the peace of God, which transcends all understanding, will guard your hearts and your minds in Christ Jesus" (Philippians 4:6-7).

5

LEAF SCARS

The Art of Living Scarfully

"God will not look you over for medals, degrees, or diplomas, but for scars." -Elbert Hubbard

Imagine a designer label that reads: *Body by God: Scars Included.* Five to be exact: one in each hand and foot and a jagged spear imprint across the rib cage. I can't help but wonder why God, who conducted the grand miracle of the resurrection, brought Jesus' body back in an imperfect state. Why not just erase the scars, and present him whole, without the gore? To return him to earth scarred seems imperfect to me—sort of a halfway healing. Was it just a partial miracle? Hadn't Jesus been through enough?

Why? Because scars tell stories. Scars are life's traumas recorded on our skin. Those fresh, red wounds etched on Jesus' hands, feet, and side are evidence that he lived. And died. And scarred. We see in Jesus an object lesson of the experiential kind. Thomas believed because of his scars, and we are saved through his scars. By choosing to leave very real and evident scars on Jesus' resurrected body, God gave us visual proof that, though Jesus died, he lives. To scar is to live!

In our lives we scar. We scratch. We dent. But we also heal. Scars are tangible reminders of wounds healed and they occur as a natural part of the body's healing process. When a layer of skin is damaged, the biological process of wound repair occurs. At the point of injury, the skin cannot rebuild itself exactly as it was. Instead, new cells emerge and old cells regroup. The skin is recreated and a scar is born.

Trees also experience protective scarring. Each fall, deciduous trees must part with their leaves. Scarlet, crimson and gold: they fall. Did you know that after losing a leaf, the plant must seal the wound? The result is a scar.

Rewind your mind to the dramatic act of the leaf separating from the tree. Leaves, in order to preserve the tree that gave it life, literally cut themselves off from the benefactor so as to do them no harm. Or something similar. Biologically speaking, this sacrificial act is called abscission. Can you hear the word *scissors* embedded within this word? *Abscission* comes from Latin: *ab* means "away," and *scindere* means "to cut."

While literary artists tend to romanticize the season of fall, I like the perspective of "detective" botanist Peter Raven, who spins the event as a murder mystery of sorts. The annual botanical "crime time" question is this: "Did he fall, or was he pushed?"[1] According to Raven, the leaf was pushed. The offender? A little rotund, donut shaped dude who severed the leaf's life-giving supply of water and nutrients thereby weakening the connection between the leaf and the stem. Once these intruder cells begin to terminate the connection, the leaf is literally left hanging. With the briefest hint of a breeze, or wisp of a bird's wing, the leaf is dealt the final blow, falling to its death by disconnection. Talk about a new perspective on the "romantic" version of fall. Perhaps the season of fall should be re-named "push."

Whether you espouse the poetic and sacrificial act of leaf fall, or the more decadent, murderous approach of Raven, the point is, leaves do fall. It's all very natural in a "naturey" sort of way. The tree doesn't pull this off (pun intended) by willing or thinking it. God created the mechanism which allows deciduous trees to survive the winter. So each fall, that tender leaf with its water-soaked veins and organs must go or be damaged by freezing temperatures. It may seem a bit expensive to produce a new leaf each spring, but it beats the alternative of freezing to death.

Post leaf loss, the tree forms a protective scar which seals off the tubes and vessels that feed the leaf. Within the leaf scar are bundle scars—tiny dots or bumps that mark where the veins entered the leaf from the stem. Interestingly, these "scar prints" are specific to each tree, a fingerprint if you will, each with a characteristic shape—ranging from round, oval, heart, or crescent shaped. Together, the shape of the leaf scar and the arrangement and number of bundle scars provide clues to a tree's identity, especially valuable during the naked or leafless season.

Consider some interesting specimens: While at first glance, the scar of the catalpa tree may appear mundane, with its simple round scar, yet with their sunken form, it takes on the appearance of a twig studded with suction cups. Or the maple tree with its crescent-moon-shaped scar pierced with three bundle scars. Or the white ash tree with its smiley-faced leaf scar. But my favorite comes in the image of the butternut leaf scar: a

LEAF SCAR AND TWIG

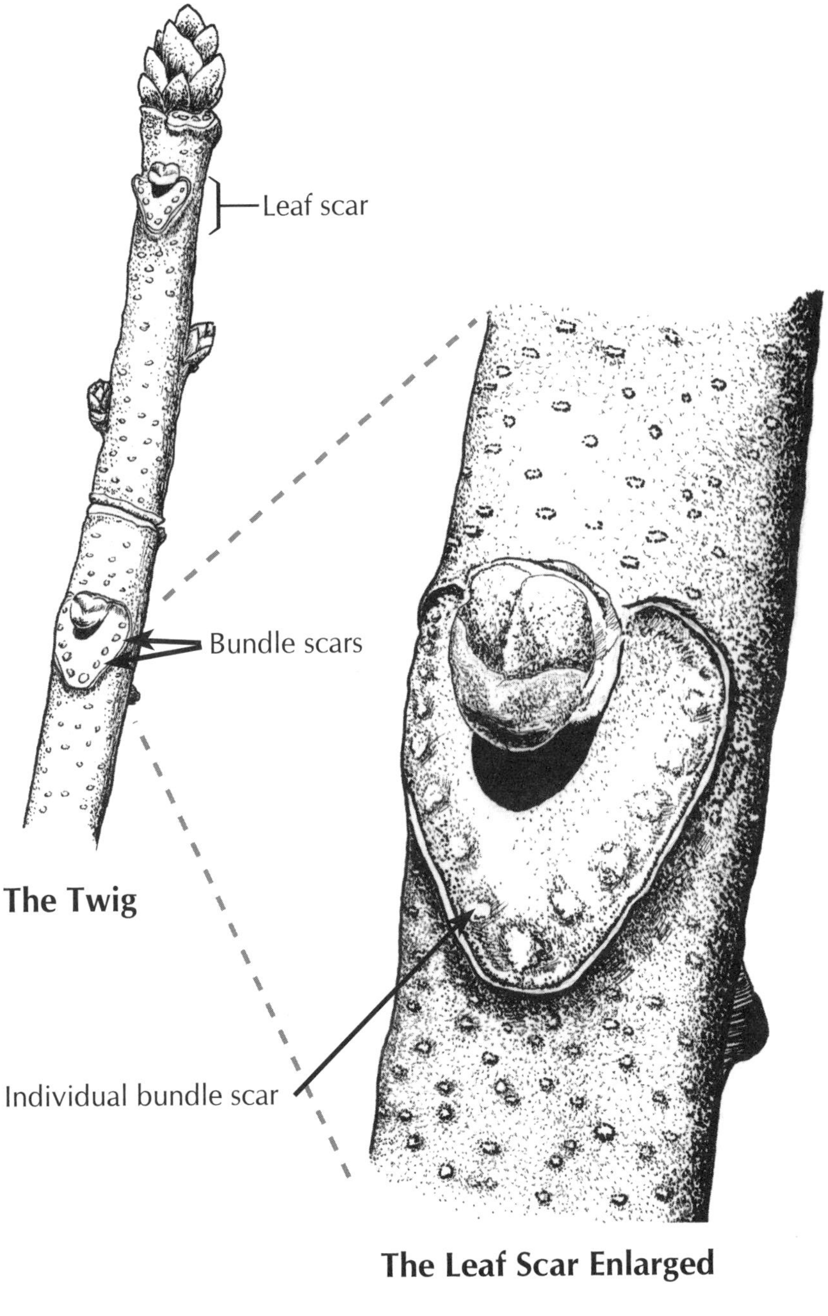

heart-shaped face sporting fuzzy eyebrows above the leaf scar.

As leaf scars define a tree, spiritual scars can define our lives. Sometimes in the process of real life, our hearts are gouged. One of my first heart scars came early in life, at age ten. On the dawn of a winter's morn the news of the death of my father cut deeply. The innocence of childhood was scarred forever. No more laughter at the dinner table, showing off muscles and milk mustaches. No more backyard gardens planting seeds of hope. No more Saturday trips to the dump followed by a dozen Winchell's doughnuts. I mourned the loss of my father for years to come—especially at my high school graduation, my marriage, and the birth of my firstborn.

Yet the loss of my father drew me closer to family. My mother became my best friend. My father's mother my mentor. My mother's parents became a lifeline I clung to. But due to the loss of my father I entered marriage at the age of twenty-two deeply scarred. I feared abandonment. As such, I clung to my spouse, my best friend. For the first years of marriage, I panicked that Terry would die. I feared when he traveled, feared when he climbed; I even feared when he closed his eyes at night. I did not want to be left again. The scar of abandonment cut deep.

I eventually came to realize that the only One who will never leave or forsake us is God. Everyone else is human. And scarred. And doomed to die. To expect a spouse, a child, or a friend to provide our joy is flawed thinking. It only leads to disappointment. God alone must be our strength, our joy, our all. I learned to cling to God and to give my husband freedom to explore and live life with abandon. As I write these words, my dear husband and I have celebrated thirty-one years of marriage, surviving his daring lifestyle of adventure and even a melanoma diagnosis.

In the act of living scarfully, we open ourselves to risk, disappointment, and hurt. In the childhood classic, *The Velveteen Rabbit*, Skin Horse explains this perfectly:

> 'Real isn't how you are made,' said the Skin Horse. 'It's a thing that happens to you. When a child loves you for a long, long time, not just to play with but REALLY loves you, then you become Real.'
>
> 'Does it hurt?' asked the Rabbit.
>
> 'Sometimes,' said the Skin Horse, for he was always truthful. 'When you are Real you don't mind being hurt.'
>
> 'Does it happen all at once, like being wound up, or bit by bit?'
>
> 'It doesn't happen all at once. You become. It takes a long time. That's why it doesn't happen often to people who break easily, or who

> have sharp edges, or who have to be carefully kept. Generally, by the time you are Real, most of your hair has been loved off, and your eyes drop out and you get loose in your joints and very shabby. But these things don't matter at all, because once you are Real, you can't be ugly, except to people who don't understand.[2]

Life lived honestly and vulnerably, hurts. Christians often wonder why God allows pain. I like what author and theologian C.S. Lewis says of pain: "Pain hurts. That is what the word means. I am only trying to show that the old Christian doctrine of being made perfect through suffering is not incredible. To prove it palatable is beyond my design."[3]

Touché, Lewis! Many people can't understand how a good and loving God would allow such pain and suffering. But pain—wretched, searing, gnawing pain—though awful, can serve a greater purpose.

When days are free of pain, we tend to dance through life, marveling at our own goodness. However, at the first pinch of pain, we squirm. Only when the pain increases to take away breath levels do we seek out the great physician and beg him to remove the pain. Perhaps God hasn't heard from us in years. Suddenly he has our undivided, screaming attention. The truth is, life hurts. Real life does come with pain and suffering. But we must learn to see life's scars of pain as rainbows reflecting through the rain. Pain has purpose.

Dr. Paul Brand, physician and author, called pain a gift. Brand taught that it creates awareness in the body that causes a reaction to flee from hurtful situations. Pain is what sparks that instinctive reflex that screams for the hand to move when it contacts a searing hot stove. Dr. Brand lived a real, scar-filled life surrounded with the suffering of others. Growing up as the son of missionaries in India, Dr. Brand witnessed the reality and value of pain first hand—in lepers. People with Hansen's disease (lepers) have lost the ability to feel pain. Their limbs are numb to the pain signals that would cause them to withdraw and ultimately results in tissue damage and limb malformations. Seeing this suffering moved Dr. Brand to make a difference.

Dr. Brand became a world-renowned hand surgeon, often restoring function and always restoring dignity to scarred individuals. He was a Christian known for his compassion, humility, and commitment to service. Dr. Brand saw the patient not as a number, but as a person to whom he longed to give comfort. Friend and colleague Eddie Askew said of Dr. Brand:

> He never concentrated solely on the hand or foot he held so gently and intimately. He looked at the patient's face, looked into the eyes, Paul was concerned for the individuals and their personalities...[4]

That is how God sees us in our suffering. I imagine God looking into our faces, longing to remove our pain. Yet he resists. He chooses to let it be, for in our pain, in the testing of our faith, we develop perseverance.

> Perseverance must finish its work so that you may be mature, and complete, not lacking anything (James 1:4).

Just as the tree must push away its leaves before the winter freeze, so too, we must prune the leaves (attitudes, behaviors, and actions) that threaten to harm our spiritual lives. That pruning is painful, yet necessary. And we scar. It is through these scars that God renews us. God has the power to heal our hurts and put us back on the road to life, a little tougher, hopefully wiser and with more understanding of ourselves and others.

In life, our spiritual scars tell survival stories. So be bold; share your story. That's the art of living scarfully. Fear not. God has excised the shame. Only the scar remains. Wear it well.

WONDERCISE

Twig Time

I love the word *twig*. Found on the same page of the dictionary as *twang, twerp* and *twinkle,* the word *twig* dwells among some of my personal favorites. It is defined as "a small shoot or branch, usually without its leaves." A tree looms large, yet the twig, in its nakedness, is often overlooked. Even so, twigs are essential to trees. Let's take a look.

Knapsack Needs:

- Hand lens
- *Woody Plants in Winter* by E. Core & N. Ammons (optional)

Survey your neighborhood trees for a twig, a branch with no leaves. Using your hand lens, find the point of leaf detachment—the leaf scar. This may be easier if you first gently detach an existing leaf from a branch; that mark you see where the leaf once was is the leaf scar. Notice the shape of the leaf scar. What shape is it? Round? Heart? Crescent? Can you see evidence of the life-sustaining veins that delivered water to the thirsty leaf? Sketch the leaf scar in your notebook.

Touch the leaf scar. Gently run your finger over the marking. As you do, realize that the scar represents not just a leaf lost, but a wound healed. And remember that in losing the leaf, the tree was protected from harm. Thanks be to God, for by his wounds we are healed.

Promise of Hope

"You have taken off your old self with its practices and put on the new self, which is being renewed in knowledge in the image of its Creator" (Colossians 3:9b-10).

PART II
Gifts of the Air

"When once you have tasted flight, you will forever walk the earth with your eyes turned skyward, for there you have been, and there you will always long to return."

–Leonardo Da Vinci

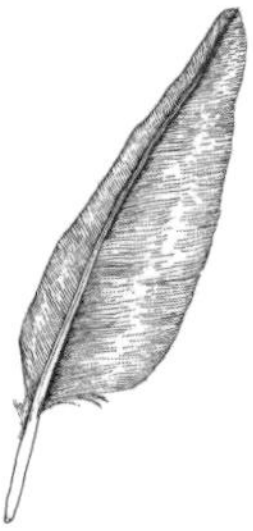

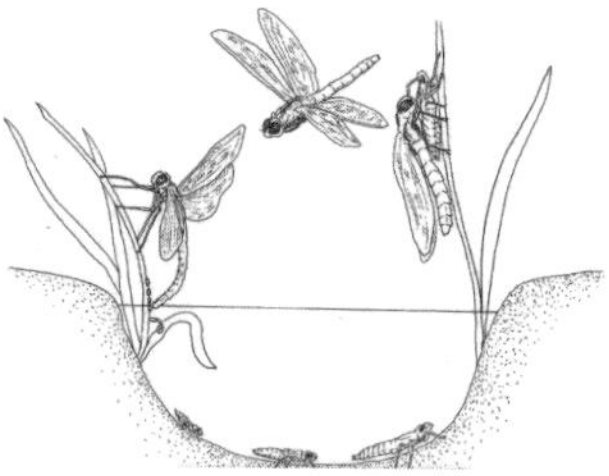

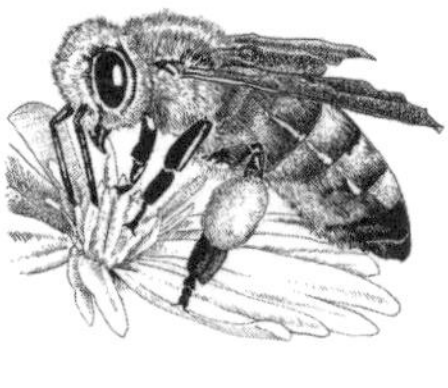

6

BIRD WINGS
Flight, Feathers, & Faith

"The reason birds can fly and we can't is simply that they have perfect faith, for to have faith is to have wings."
–Sir James Matthew Barrie

Careening across the bay in an airboat monitoring shorebird usage in Willapa Bay, I smiled. It was a balmy, sixty-four-degree spring day, a rare occurrence in April on the Washington coast. I congratulated myself on selecting such a fine day for this assignment (Yeah, I know, pride goeth before a fall!).

Spotting a flock of close to seven hundred shorebirds in the distance, I motioned to the driver to follow the birds. Wind in my hair and binoculars at my brow, we zoomed in for a closer look. Suddenly the airboat slammed into a bank of mud. As I flew out of the airboat, the birds on the mudflat took flight, leaving me lying flat on my back in a sea of mud, thinking, *If only I could fly, I would have soared.*

Humans have longed to fly for centuries. Our fascination with flight is legendary. Consider the story of Daedalus, of Greek mythology fame, who longed to fly to escape his prison. Daedalus fashioned wings from wax and feathers for himself and for his son Icarus. Sweet escape turned sour when Daedalus lost altitude and was dashed into the rocks. Icarus dared to fly too high and encountered the searing heat of the sun. With melted wings, Icarus sank to his death in the sea below.

Another classical legend tells of Alexander the Great and the great griffin, the mythical creature with the body and tail of a lion and the head and wings of an eagle. Longing to fly, Alexander is said to have captured a pair of griffins, harnessed them to his throne and tamed the wild beasts. On the wings of griffins, Alexander took to the skies.

And the flight fantasy continued with the tale of the ninth century B.C. British king Bladud who donned a pair of homemade wings only to be dashed to death in the failed flight attempt. Super stories with superman ideas, these dreams would remain fantasy until the brilliant scientist and inventor Leonardo da Vinci arrived on scene.

In 1485 A.D. Leonardo seems to have been the first solid link joining the imagination of flight to the actual experimentation with flight. After countless hours of bird observation, Leonardo devised theories of flight based on wind resistance, and its effect on the bird wing which he documented in his "Codex of Flight." His observations resulted in the bird-inspired design of a precursor to the modern helicopter which Leonardo called the Ornithopter (really—it's a word!).

Today, the process of deriving inspiration for invention from nature observation has earned a fancy name—Biomimetics: "the mimicking of biological structures, behaviors and processes to create cutting-edge technologies."[1] Wilbur Wright, of the flight brothers' fame, practiced the art of biomimetics. According to National Park Service writer David Andrews, Wilbur

> pedaled to a place called the Pinnacles, eerie outcrops where buzzards and hawks dove and darted in the heights above the Miami River ... Will saw that, hit by a gust, birds reasserted their balance with a slight twist of the wingtips.[2]

Boom. See the flash of idea? From watching the Creator's handcrafted, one-of-a-kind wonder bird, Wilbur grabbed hold of the key that would unlock the secret of flight and achieve his dream, creating a source of mechanized flight for man.

Because Wilbur was the son of a bishop in the Church of the United Brethren, I can't help but wonder whether he was influenced by these words in Job 12:7:

> But ask the animals, and they will teach you, or the birds of the air, and they will tell you ...

While we may never know the answer to this, we do know that the birds didn't read a book on flight. They just flew. The book of Genesis tells us,

> Let the birds fly above the earth across the expanse of the sky. So God

created … every winged bird according to its kind (Genesis 1:20-21).

The fact that birds fly is a wonder. Let's look at some of the intricacies of avian aerodynamics.

To take to the air, a bird must overcome two natural forces: gravity, that which keeps us grounded, and drag, the force which slows things down. Remember sticking your hand out the window as a child while traveling in a car? That simple act demonstrates drag. When your hand is cupped, you can catch the air; when you turn your hand flat and horizontal, your hand slices through the air.

In the miracle of flight, the shape of the wing affects drag and allows lift-off. Envision a cross section of a bird's wing. See the inflated comma lying on its side? This shape is called an airfoil. Birds actually use air pressure to fly. If you don't believe in air pressure, consider what happens when you blow up a balloon. You are filling the balloon with air, which exerts pressure on the balloon, and the air outside the balloon presses back. The air inside the balloon has pressure. The term "floating on air" takes on a new meaning when you consider the art of flying.

When air meets the edge of an airfoil, it splits into two streams of air—one whooshing over the curved top of the wing, the second stream passing slower underneath the straighter side of the wing. The air passing above the wing goes faster (creating lower air pressure) than the layer below (higher pressure). This change in air pressure is what causes lift. Imagine the lower pressure above as an invisible force sucking the bird upward, and the now greater air pressure below the wing pressing upward. These pressure changes work together to give the bird what we call "lift." And the bird rises.

See for yourself. Take a sheet of paper cut to about two by eight inches. Insert about three inches of the paper "wing" in a book (like you would insert a bookmark) and close the book, with a five inch flap sticking out.

Now hold the book at mouth level and blow across the cover of the book in the direction of the paper strip, which is hanging down on the other side due to gravity. As you blow, you increase the speed of the air passing over the top of the paper, which reduces the air pressure. Now the air pressure below the paper is greater, hence the paper wing lifts up. Congratulations. You just performed a basic physics experiment and demonstrated the physical law known as the Bernoulli Principle: greater air speed lowers air pressure.

Now that we understand the basic mechanics of the wing and its contribution to flight, let's dissect the wing and encounter the wonder of the feather.

Feathers are unique to birds, and all birds have feathers. Feathers function in protection, insulation, and mate attraction. And of course, feathers are the building blocks of flight. Without feathers, birds would be grounded. And naked.

In his infinite wisdom, God organized and placed the feathers on the bird in a most amazing way. Next time you prepare a chicken for dinner, spend a minute or two looking for the pits, or follicles, in the skin of the bird (this may seem odd, but welcome to the biologist's world). This pit is the point of attachment between the bird's feather and its body. While birds appear to be a covered with a chaotic mass of feathers, the feathers are actually arranged neatly in tracts—lines from which the feathers grow, overlapping like shingles on a roof. Thus, the bird is covered.

Yet, combing through the mass of fluff, we find that not all feathers are alike. Just as you sport different garments for different purposes, birds have several feather types, each with a specific purpose. The three basic types are down, contour, and flight feathers.

Bird "underwear," if I may be so bold, is the down feather, which insulates. A bird's form and fashion are found in the contour feather, which provides shape and color. Finally, flight feathers provide the ability to soar. Other less common types of feathers are semiplume, filoplume, and bristle.

A feather can be divided into three sections—quill, body, and barbs. The quill, that cylindrical, transparent and hollow portion of the feather—its "handle," so to speak—is where the rubber meets the road, or where the feather meets the body. The tiny opening at the tip is called the umbilicus (etymologically related to the term which defines the cord that anchored us to our mothers). This point of attachment is necessary for nourishment of the feather as it grows. Once formed, the umbilicus seals off and the feather becomes analogous to your fingernail—dead material that can be trimmed without feeling.

Next is the body of the feather, consisting of a leaf-like shaft and vane. The shaft is the central vein-like structure that bisects the feather. On either side of the shaft, extend the flexible vanes of the feather. Keep in mind that only the quill and the vane of the feather can be seen with the naked eye.

Finally, branching off of the vane is a series of parallel branches, called barbs. In a process similar to that of Russian *matryoshka* (nesting) dolls, each barb gives rise to a smaller version of the same structure. This view

FEATHER

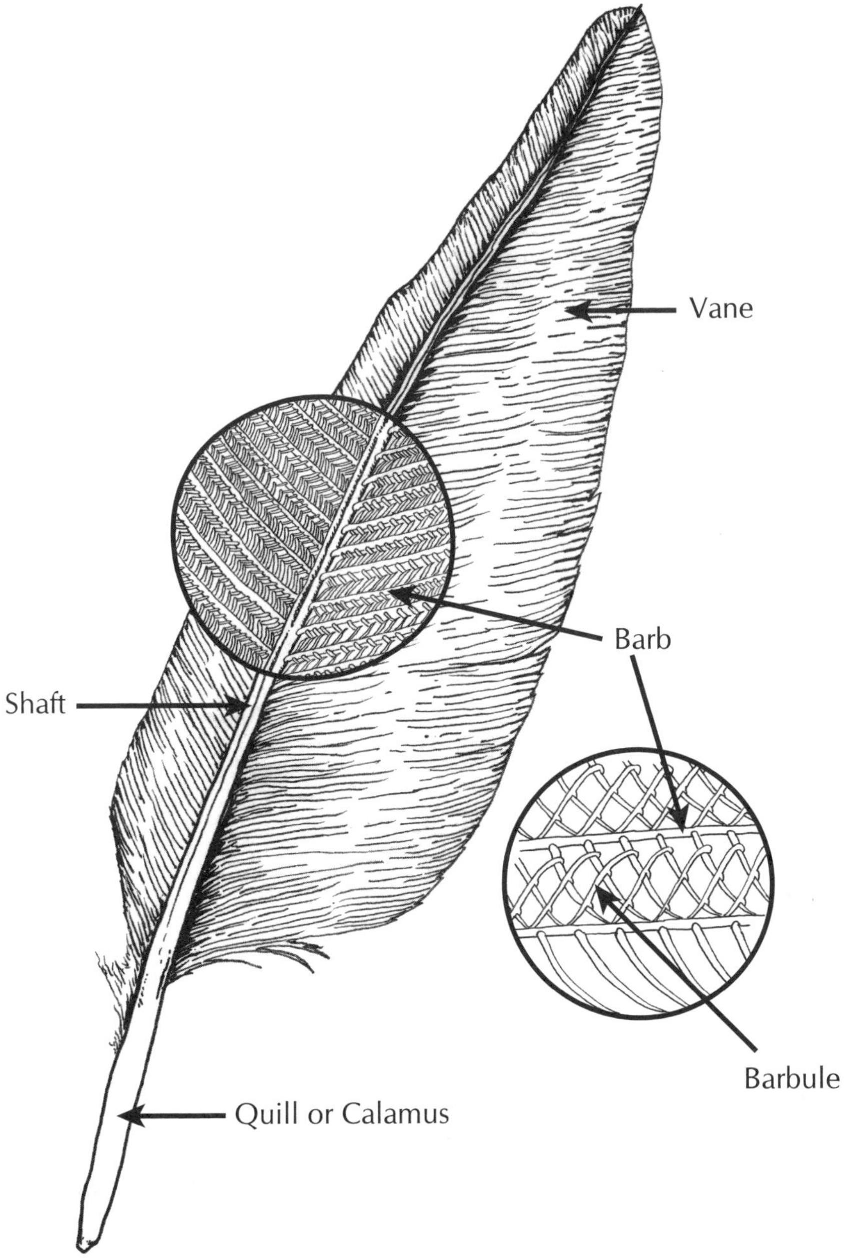
Vane
Barb
Shaft
Barbule
Quill or Calamus

from inside the feather reveals an intricate, ingenious system of barbs and barbules (hooklets). Think Velcro here. The vane is composed of many mini Velcro zippers of sorts, each containing a series of interlocking hooks and barbs which link together to give the feather flex and rigidity at the same time. Imagine hundreds of individual plume-like soldiers snapping to attention, locking the barbs into a fortified feather front.

The remarkable construction of the feather should give us pause. Its structure demonstrates strength with flexibility. Strength with flexibility plays an important role in the lives of humans as well. If we are to soar in this life, we would do well to mimic the structure of the feather. Our faith is our strength. And that faith hangs not on the flimsy barb of our spiritual lives, but is inexorably linked to the powerful grasp of the Master's outstretched hand that saves and strengthens us.

Sometimes in life, the feathers of our faith get ruffled. Consider the confident, passionate, and driven Wilbur Wright. Just two years shy of accomplishing one of the greatest feats of all time, he almost threw in the wing, er … towel. One could say his flight feathers were ruffled with doubt.

After experiencing a major setback in his theory on lift, Tom Crouch, author of *The Bishop's Boys*, describes Wilbur in a state of profound doubt and shaky self confidence.

> Wilbur wondered whether two years of time, money and effort had been wasted. More to the point, if they decided to continue the work, what should they do next? They were willing to accept an error in the lift tables, but how were they to correct it? And how could they overcome the difficulty with the lateral control system?[3]

Sometimes the questions in our lives seem to outnumber the solutions. But while we long for answers, real satisfaction and adventure comes in living the questions—moving through times of uncertainty when the way is unclear. The Wright brothers pressed on when they could have stopped. Two years later, they soared to success. The telegram to their father says it best:

> Success four flights Thursday morning # all against twenty-one mile wind started from Level with engine power alone # average speed through air thirty one miles longest 57 (sic) seconds inform Press Home #### Christmas. Orville Wright[4]

What is not mentioned in the telegram is that after those four successful flights, the final flight attempt of the day ended in disaster. Their amazing airplane, caught by a gust of wind, sought to soar solo. Photographer John T. Daniels jumped up to stop it and ended up flying along with the craft, dangling by an arm. The startled and screaming Daniels hung on as he watched the engine break loose, and the crippled craft rolled over upside down, dumping Daniels into the dust. Remarkably, Daniels survived the first recorded airplane crash uninjured. The world's first airplane did not.

On its day of infamy the craft lay in a crumpled mass of wood and wire, along with the Wright brothers' hopes and dreams. To achieve their dream of sustained flight, their hardest work lay ahead of them. Perhaps they needed to preen.

Preening is a process birds use to keep feathers in top condition. Drawing its beak through its feathers, a bird can remove dirt and grime and align each feather to its optimal position for flight. Un-preened feathers don't fly so well, just as a neglected faith leaves us floundering. Daily we need the touch of the master's hand to restore our tired and tattered feathers of faith. When we connect with God through the disciplines of prayer and reading his Word and commit our lives to discipleship, we are preening our faith. And a preened faith is a flying faith.

Life is filled with turbulence. We mustn't be afraid. We must leave the comfort zone of our nest and follow our dreams. Is this a slice of "pie in the sky" rhetoric? Not at all. You're holding my dream in your hands. This book was born from years of prayer—plus heaps of difficult, painful work. And my faith is richer for it. Pursuing our dreams enhances our faith. But don't take my word for it, read Hebrews chapter 11 for a list of dream believers—and achievers. A dreamless faith is a dull faith. And a faithless dream is doomed.

What is on your dream list?:

- Write your memoir?
- Memorize scripture?
- Start a home for pregnant teens?
- Get that college degree?
- Work in the field of your passion?
- Play the guitar?

- Join the Peace Corps?
- Read through the Bible in a year?

Dreams don't materialize on wishful thinking alone. First, we must commit.

> Commit to the LORD whatever you do, and your plans will succeed (Proverbs 16:3).

Then take action.

From the comfort zone of our nest, we must teeter to the edge and take the leap. Flap and fly—sometimes wobbly, sometimes wonderfully. The point is we must try. Exercise your wings of faith. With God, all things are possible.

WONDERCISE

The Art of Feather Observation

If, as Mark Twain said, "Clothes make the man," then feathers must make the bird. Let's investigate the structure of the flight feather and take some time to watch a bird in flight.

Knapsack Needs:

- Flight feather of a bird (from nature or a craft store)
- Hand lens
- Binoculars

1. Study the feather. Notice the three primary parts of the feather—the quill, the body (vane), and the barbs, the individual plumes which comprise the vane.

2. Bend the feather and examine the way the feather reacts. Do the barbs hold together or separate? Toss the feather into the air and watch its descent.

3. Look at the feather through the hand lens while separating the individual barbs with your fingernail. Gently push them back together and watch them "magnetically" jump back together—this is the mechanism of the Velcro-like hook and barb coming together.

Take time this week to observe a bird in flight. Contemplate the concept of lift. Remember that flight is dependent upon air pressure. No pressure, no flight. Allow God to use the pressures of life to lift you higher and closer to him.

Promise of Hope

"The Lord is the everlasting God, the creator of the ends of the earth … He gives strength to the weary and increases the power of the weak. Even youths grow tired and weary, and young men stumble and fall, but those who hope in the Lord will renew their strength. They will soar on wings like eagles; they will run and not grow weary, they will walk and not be faint" (Isaiah 40:28-31).

7

THE DRAGONFLY

Lowlife Larva to Acrobatic Adult

"Nature often holds up a mirror so we can see more clearly the ongoing processes of growth, renewal and transformation in our lives." -Anonymous

Dragonflies mirror change. Dragonfly larva, that is. In a series of life changing molts, the dragonfly babe ultimately emerges from its aquatic underworld, crawls to the shore of adulthood and unzips the last vestiges of immaturity in exchange for its final form—a winged acrobatic wonder.

Change happens. In insects as well as humans. Or at least it should. God desires growth and renewal in our lives. Life is to be a series of transformations to develop Christlike behaviors. And while I like the thought of becoming a better me, oftentimes I am hesitant to welcome change. A better description of my encounter with this visitor called Change is to grudgingly accept it. I'd prefer to experience change butterfly style—where I enter the privacy of my cocoon, encapsulate all my bad habits, and *poof!* in one fell swoop I emerge a full-fledged mature Christian.

Unfortunately, life doesn't work that way. My metamorphosis occurs gradually in a series of stages, over a period of years. One by one, I shed behaviors that hold me captive. And much like the dragonfly, I transition bit by bit into a better me. A more complete me. A more Christlike me. Let's explore the topic of transformation through the mysterious and marvelous life of a dragonfly.

Have you looked at a dragonfly recently? Scratch that. Have you looked at a dragonfly ever? Really looked? Explored the beauty of its intricate lace-like wings (dragonfly species can be separated by subtle differences in wing venation alone)? Contemplated the complexity of its multi-faceted eyes that seem to swallow its head and follow your every move? Enjoyed the antics of a dragonfly in flight? The adult form is downright spectacular. The aquatic larval form not so much, at least upon first glance. But dragonfly larvae (called nymphs) are impressive in their own right.

From head to tail, dragonfly larvae are marvels. At the head end, larvae are endowed with a harpoon-like, hinged jaw (labium) which they shoot out to seize prey. And while they appear primitive, their movement is remarkably advanced—using aquatic jet propulsion. Larvae draw in water through gills tucked into their abdomen. In cartoon style, they squirt a jet stream of water from their rectum which propels them forward. What a creative God we have!

Some may find the larval dragonfly form more frightful than delightful. Yet from this mis-shapen and curmudgeonly fierce creature blossoms the powerful, aerial acrobat. How does such a transformation occur? Since most of us are familiar with the life cycle of the butterfly, let's begin there and edit for the dragonfly version. The butterfly cycle of life moves through four stages: egg, caterpillar, pupa (cocoon), and butterfly. This is called "complete metamorphosis" in the insect world of entomology. The dragonfly does it in three stages. As such, dragonflies are slapped with the less charming label of "incomplete metamorphosis" because they lack one key stage: the pupae, that stage where change occurs in the privacy of a cocoon. Under the cloak of darkness. Private. Sheltered. But unfortunately for the dragonfly, that's not the way it morphs. Read on.

In the beginning, the aerial adult dragonfly hovers over the face of the deep (cue the drumroll as dragonfly drama unfolds on the big screen of your mind). The female dragonfly, ripe with eggs, must carefully deposit the seed of the next generation. The art of egg laying varies with species. There seems to be more than one way to lay an egg. And ecological factors play a role.

For example, research shows one waterfall-dwelling dragonfly species alters its egg-laying technique depending upon the rate of the current. When the current moved at high speeds (670m3 per second), the eggs were laid "in the spray zone" with "females sticking eggs onto the layer of roots and bryzoa covering rocks." Yet at lower current speeds the same species "only rarely attached eggs from a settled position, and even then directly into the river itself."[1]

There are a myriad of egg laying modes, from skimming over the

LIFE CYCLE OF DRAGONFLY

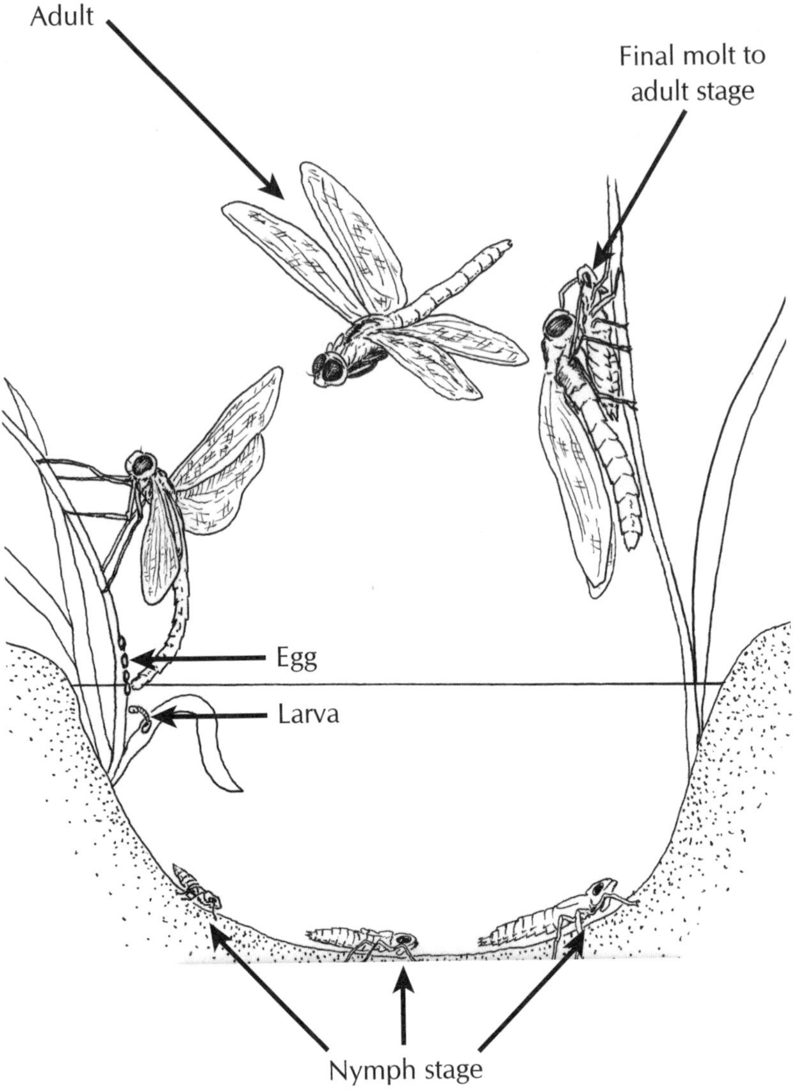

surface of the waters dipping its "PEZ dispenser" abdomen into the pond, to the B-52 bomber-style airdrop (releasing its eggs in flight directly over the water), to the more labor intensive method of injecting eggs into leaves. Whatever the creativity of the method, eggs are laid.

Once in the water, the egg hatches into an immature larval stage—a creature so small it could fit inside the period at the end of this sentence. In this first stage of life, although it is

> unable to walk or swim, [it] is specialized for travel (by jumping) between the egg-laying site and the microhabitat of the free-living larva, and it usually lasts no longer than the time needed to accomplish this short journey.[2]

The miracle of this detail is not lost on me. Even in the microscopic beginning of a dragonfly's life, such minute details—such as scooching from point A to point B without wings or legs—are taken care of. Amazing. Simply amazing.

Continued growth requires a process called molting, which is the shedding of their skin. Dragonflies (and insects in general) are saddled with an exoskeleton-—a hardened, shell-like version of skin that prevents growth unless they escape this entrapment. While in the nymph stage, which can last from two months to ten years depending on species, the dragonfly passes through a series of successive molts (ranging from nine to seventeen times) and eventually reaches adulthood.[3]

Until the final molt, life in the underwater world of dragonfly babes plays like a B-grade horror movie: the larva lives the life of a cutthroat carnivore, preying upon the likes of mosquito larvae, worms, tadpoles and even small fish. Frankly, the whole voracious and violent larval thing reminds me of Saul before he was called Paul. Saul was fierce. Saul killed Christians. Yet Saul experienced a remarkable molt. To call it dramatic would be an understatement.

Paul himself describes his Sauline days:

> I too was convinced that I ought to do all that was possible to oppose the name of Jesus of Nazareth. And that is just what I did in Jerusalem … I put many of the saints in prison, and when they were put to death, I cast my vote against them.… In my obsession against them, I even went to foreign cities to persecute them (Acts 26:9-11).

Saul was imprisoned in the darkness of his hatred for Christians. God was about to change that. God zapped him on the road to Damascus with a blinding flash of light. Saul crashed to the ground and heard a thunderous voice. "Saul, Saul, why do you persecute me?" I can't begin to imagine the complete panic and confusion Saul experienced in that moment. After his incessant persecution of the church—his indifference and hatred of Christians—Saul is suddenly blinded by a flash of supernatural light and comes face to face with the holy God. I shudder at the thought.

Saul asks, "Who are you, Lord?" Sort of a pointless question. Saul, educated in rabbinic tradition, knew that such a heavenly voice had to be God himself, to say nothing of that supernatural light.

As Saul struggles up from the ground, he opens his eyes to see midnight darkness at high noon. Immersed into three days of blindness, Saul begins a new stage of life. A larval stage, if you will. Saul is shedding his old way of life. And in a dragonfly kind of way, Saul begins a series of transformations that will unveil a new version of himself. A powerful presence in the kingdom of God. Based on his own dramatic renewal, Paul challenged others to experience the cleansing that godly transformation yields:

> Do not conform any longer to the pattern of this world, but be transformed by the renewing of your mind.... Therefore, if anyone is in Christ, he is a new creation; the old has gone, the new has come!... I preached that they should repent and turn to God and prove their repentance by their deeds (Romans 12:2, 2 Corinthians 5:17, Acts 26:20).

Paul knew radical, life-changing transformation. Who better to challenge us to change than the man who experienced transformation firsthand? I find my own road to transformation rooted in his. My eyes were opened to this concept while writing this very chapter.

One day while working on the tenth draft of this chapter (okay, third, but it felt like more) I hit a roadblock. Bits of information lay strewn about my mind like jigsaw puzzle pieces, and I couldn't connect them. I couldn't even find the edge pieces to order the paragraphs. It was a mess. So I ran.

Seeking clarity, I laced up my Asics and jogged up the road. For five miles I ran, pondering concepts, seeking order, and considering application. Nothing worked. Nearing home, I spied something black in the dust at the side of the road. A bandana. *Could come in handy on a hike,* I thought. I bent down and snatched it up. That's when I noticed. Emblazoned across the bandana were tiny images of skulls—those ugly, screaming-death kind of skull and crossbones insignia. I flung the harbinger of death to the ground. I hated death and all that it stood for. Finality and loss. Pain and suffering. Then all at once it struck me. Death of old ways is the missing piece of the puzzle. Dragonflies face death with each shed. They die to a larval stage that constricts them, experience new growth and enter the next stage. Without death, what is life? Gingerly, I picked up the bandana again and pondered the concept of death.

Death, in a sense, is what gave life to this chapter and book. Death of my will, my expectations, and my fears. Each shedding was a process. And each shedding was difficult. Shedding my fears has been the most painful. Imprisoned by unfounded fears, I languished in my cocoon of doubt and unbelief. I needed freedom. I needed Jesus in a new way. I had held him at arm's length, just outside my prison doors. I needed to break free. After all, Jesus came "to open eyes that are blind, free captives from prison and to release from dungeons those who sit in darkness" (Isaiah 42:7) In my doubt and confusion, life was dark.

I wasn't trapped by the big Ds of divorce, death, disaster; my prison was self-imposed and concealed in the lower-case "d." The "d" of doubt. I consoled myself with the fact that it wasn't a big "D," or a big deal. After all, doubt doesn't cripple. Or does it?

It did. In a mighty way, that little "d" of doubt imprisoned me in my fears and unbelief. You see, I did not believe in my God-given ability. Doubt is a nasty prison. I was shackled by the one who holds the d's of doubt and discouragement, satan himself. Imprisoned by his insidious chants of

> You're not good enough … You don't know what you're doing …
> You can't write!

My mind taunted me. And I believed the lies. But, you ask, aren't you a believer? Yes, of course. But I believed in jesus. Little " j" jesus. Lower case jesus. Weak and watered down jesus.

In the midst of my doubts, I met Petey Prater, a godly woman of prayer at a writer's conference. Petey gently opened my eyes to the fact that I was trapped in defeat and that I held the key to the prison of my fears. And Petey prayed for me. The larval skin that kept me trapped in anxiety, fear, and doubt split wide open. I met "Big J" Jesus and experienced that power he longs to pour into each of our lives. While the oppressive shell of fear left me, I must still do a daily cleansing of prayer to keep it from creeping back into my life.

Removing the shell of "old self" is hard. This shedding of skin hurts, makes us vulnerable. But this process is necessary. For what is life if it is not a continual molting, bringing us closer and closer to that final stage, the imago (in entomological terms). Restricted by those old skins of habit, transformation occurs to liberate us. When it is time, God opens the door and ushers us out. Out of doubt. Out of darkness. Out of denial. But we must endure. And wait for him. We cannot break free without the key. God is that key.

Sometimes I just want to sidestep the shedding. Paul addressed this desire:

> For to me, to live is Christ and to die is gain. If I am to go on living in the body, this will mean fruitful labor for me. Yet what shall I choose? I do not know! I am torn between the two: I desire to depart and be with Christ, which is better by far; but it is more necessary for you that I remain in the body. Convinced of this, I know that I will remain and I will continue with all of you for your progress and joy in the faith (Philippians 1:21-25).

Wow. That's transformation. Spoken by a man who knew the pain of shedding his old skin. Paul molted Saul. As for me? I'm on the molt to maturity. Until then, I will continue to shed and split, allowing the master to reshape me into the stately being he wants me to become. That, my friend, is a "holy metamorphosis."

WONDERCISE

A Day with Dragonflies

Being in the presence of dragonflies is like stepping into past, present and future simultaneously. When I glimpse the aerial adult, I am reminded of my glorious future in heaven, yet when I peer beneath the water and find a larva, I am reminded of my daily shedding of self. And, as in a dragonfly's life, we can't have one without the other. Spend a day in the presence of dragonflies.

Knapsack Needs:

- Binoculars
- Footwear that can get wet
- Long sleeved shirt to protect if mosquitoes are present
- Sunglasses and or sunhat

Because water is essential to dragonfly development and reproduction, lakes, ponds, and streams are good places to spot a dragonfly. My favorite method is to launch my kayak from the shore of a lake in summer and paddle amongst the reeds, a playground for dragonflies. However, dragonflies can also be observed from the shore.

Just remember to move slowly, and take time to survey several habitat types: a protected seep area, an inlet, or the surface of the lake itself. Don't forget to check for dragonflies that may be perched on leaves or stems of aquatic vegetation.

After you have observed the areas above water, take some time to sit beside the water. Contemplate the place where the dragonfly begins its life—the underworld of water—and the stages it passes through before its ultimate transformation into that glorious winged adult.

May you "hear the flutter and whir of dragonfly wings … see astounding aerodynamic displays at speeds that will challenge your eye's ability to keep pace" and "regain curiosity about the small things in the universe…"[4] And I would add, give praise to the Creator for the marvelous wonder of the dragonfly.

Promise of Hope

"You were taught with regard to your former way of life, to put off your old self, which is being corrupted by its deceitful desires; to be made new in the attitude of your minds; and to put on the new self, created to be like God in true righteousness and holiness" (Ephesians 4:22-24).

8
CHASING the BLUES
On Butterflies & Moods

"Beautiful and graceful, varied and enchanting, small but approachable, butterflies lead you to the sunny side of life. And everyone deserves a little sunshine."
–Jeffrey Glassberg

One day I worshiped the Lord by chasing a butterfly in Brazil. Some people, like me, can be moved to worship by the flight of a butterfly. Mind you, this was no ordinary butterfly; this was a blue morpho, fluttering over a waterfall.

As morning dawned bright and clear in the tiny tourist town of Pocos de Caldas, Brazil, I tossed a penny into the Fountain of Desire, where the local tradition promised desires untold in exchange for a coin. Typically, I don't believe in that sort of stuff, but almost immediately I was chasing the butterfly of my dreams.

As the coin was in mid-flight, I snapped to attention when the "flying flower" fluttered into view. Hypnotized by the beat of its iridescent wings, I fell under the spell of this ephemeral creature and followed. Over creeks, under vines, around rocks, I followed. With each step, my spirit soared.

Butterfly adulation is nothing new. Butterflies have been dazzling humanity since the dawn of time, symbolizing rebirth, happiness, and joy in many cultures. Many a soul has been snagged in the net of their charm.

One interesting and surprising character who was lured by the butterfly's beauty was the literary legend Vladimir Nabokov. Perhaps best known for *Lolita*, a controversial novel of the twentieth century, Nabokov lived a second life as a passionate lepidopterist (the scientific term for one who studies butterflies). Nabokov described being in the presence of butterflies as "ecstasy … a momentary vacuum into which rushes all that I love."[1] I would concur. Butterflies are a wonder to behold.

Tradition holds that the origin of the word butterfly came from England, home to several species sporting butter-yellow wings. And the very name "Monarch butterfly" also has English history. The golden stripe adorning the top of the chrysalis reminded European settlers of the glistening crown worn by their human monarch, King James I. Bestowing the name "Monarch" on the butterfly signified a new-world tribute to an old-world king.

The gossamer garment of the butterfly—its wings—are also of a kingly nature, richly woven with the colors of royalty. When I look at the wings of a butterfly, I am reminded of the detailed instructions God gave in Exodus chapter 28 concerning the design of the ephod, a sleeveless garment of special significance worn by the high priest. Artistically worked by elite craftsmen, the ephod was created with fine linens, stunning stones, and pure gold. If God gives such concern to the creation of a priestly garment, imagine the thought that went into the detail of the butterfly wing.

The mechanism of the shimmer and shine contained in the butterfly's paper-thin wings has intrigued countless researchers over the years. Ancient Greeks are noted to have recognized the scales on the butterfly wing and given them the name *lepido-ptera*, which translates "scale-wing."

The secret to color lies in the millions of microscopic scales that blanket the wing. Quilted with blocks of slightly-overlapping, yet precisely-arranged scales, the wing is pieced together in an exquisite design. Bear in mind, the various color patterns of butterflies and the specific mechanism by which color is produced varies from species to species, but generally, scales produce color in one of two ways: either physically or structurally.

Physical color is produced by scales that have pigments embedded in the wing, which absorb certain wavelengths of light and reflect others. According to Dr. Peter Vukusic, a physicist studying iridescence in butterfly wings, "Pigmentary colour is often not very bright."[2] So the "wow" of the butterfly's flashy, brilliant iridescence is actually due to the structural color component, a different entity altogether. Let's look at this phenomenon in greater detail.

If you could peel back the surface layer of a butterfly wing and look within, you would find a complex, three dimensional array of microscopic crystal-like nanostructures (scales), sandwiched between the fragile upper

BUTTERFLY

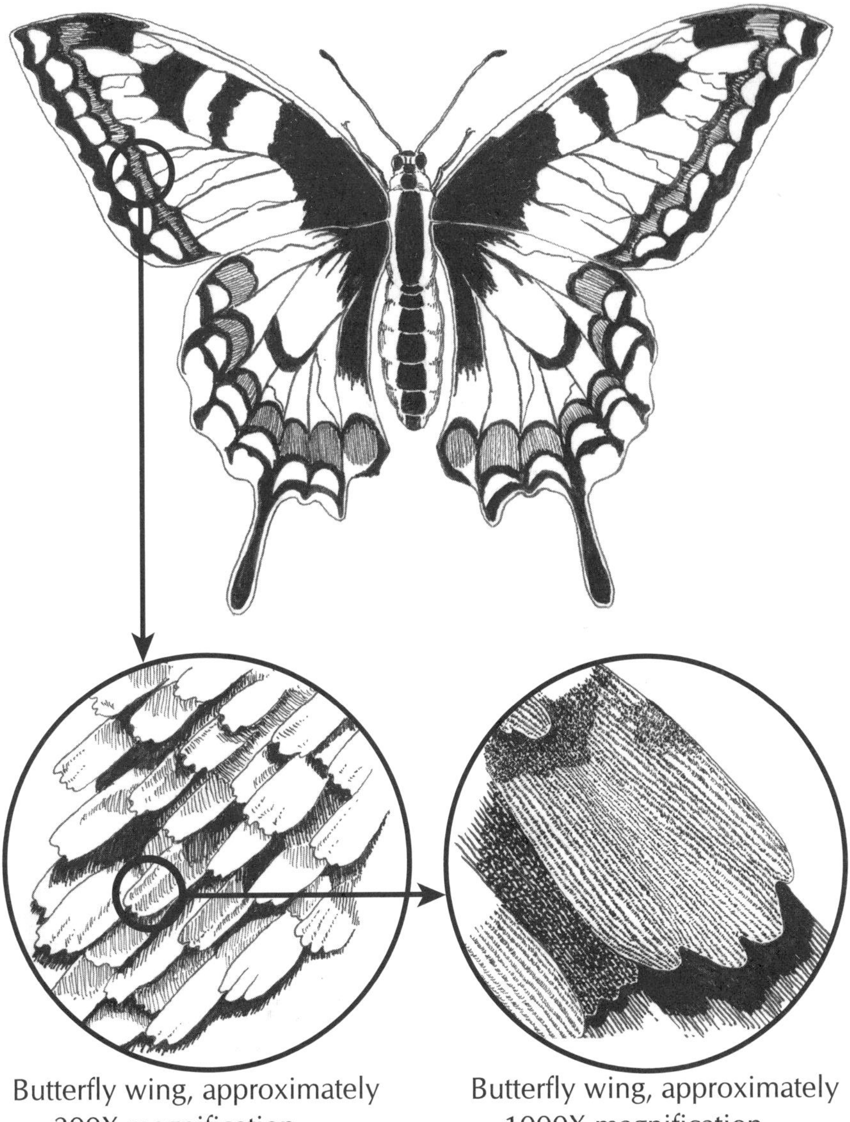

Butterfly wing, approximately 200X magnification

Butterfly wing, approximately 1000X magnification

Butterfly Wings Are Covered With Thousands Of Microscopic Overlapping Scales

and lower membrane of the wing.[3]

Nano means "billionth." A nanometer is a billionth of a meter. A micron is a millionth of a meter—unbelievably, incomprehensibly small. Nano-scientists spend their lives researching incredibly small items, one of which is the butterfly scale, approximated to be between one to three microns in size. To put this in perspective, a human hair is roughly fifty microns thick. Butterfly scales are beyond small. But their structural composition is nothing short of grand.

While the butterfly scale is small, it is anything but simple. Riddled with a complicated system of ridges and grooves, and constructed of multiple layers of chitin and air, this geometric-shaped wonder works magic in the realm of the light world, creating color out of nothing, much like the "fire" or color that sparkles from a clear diamond.

To understand the mesmerizing properties of iridescence contained within the scale, we must realize that light travels in waves. Stay with me here; we are about to enter the Land of Physics. We will go painlessly, I promise. And it might even be fun.

Defined as "a rainbow exhibition of colors," iridescence results when light of differing wavelengths is reflected multiple times from layers in the surface of a material. What is a wavelength of light, you ask? Good question.

A wavelength is the length of the repeating wave shape. Imagine a crowd of sports fans doing "the wave": a wave length is the distance between the first group of people standing with their hands stretched directly overhead to the next set of people with their hands stretched overhead. That is, begin measuring the length of the wave from the point at which the crowd has hands directly overhead (its peak) to the point at which the crowd farther down the row reaches the same position, with its hands directly overhead (end peak). This is one wave-length. Light travels in these waves, much as the crowd sends its wave through the stadium.

Now take your wavelength image to the ocean. Imagine light as waves on the ocean. See the swells of light coming in regular intervals, rolling into the shore, where they crest, and eventually break on shore. Now visualize the butterfly wing, covered with thousands of microscopic scales. When light, traveling in rolling waves of different length, crashes into the multi-layered transparent scale (the shore), it is reflected numerous times, causing a shimmer of dazzling color which our eyes drink in as iridescent and intense color.

While I would like to believe that God created the butterfly's rainbow of color solely for my enjoyment, there is another purpose to his creative craftsmanship. Color helps the butterfly with camouflage, mate attraction, and even heat absorption. Clearly, God thinks of everything.

While color plays a role in butterfly biology, consider the effect of the colors of light on human emotions. Researchers have found that blue light plays a role in regulating emotions. In addition, different colors of light can affect our moods. Blue soothes. Red excites. As clinical psychologist and author Carroll Izard notes,

> Changes in our emotions can alter the appearance of our world, from bright and cheerful to dark and gloomy...[4]

Sometimes I find myself consumed by the darkness of an emotional mood monsoon. Desperately I seek the sunlight. And the Son-Light. Nevertheless, I remain stranded in the storm of a mood. Nothing can extricate me. Not even scripture.

During thirty years of ministry, I have repeatedly encountered depressed and defeated people, chiding themselves that they just need to pray harder or pray more. Read more scripture. They labeled themselves as faith failures. Nothing could be farther from the truth. Sometimes all the praying and reading in the world may not change your mood.

Emotions are God given. And perhaps we need to stop trying to do more and just be still. Be with God in our sorrow. Be with God in our disappointment. Be with God in our funk. Remember that God ministers to us where we are. Not just where we want to be.

On the days when you are stuck in one of those I-can't-put-my-finger-on-it, there's-no-rational-reason-for-it, downright disturbing funks, stop trying so hard to extricate yourself. I used to desperately try to claw my way out of the pit of despair. No more. I have learned to embrace the emotion. Okay, so perhaps embrace is too strong a term. Try endure. Moods and their effect on my psyche can be painful. I would rather escape, but sometimes the lesson comes in the enduring. Society would not have us believe this.

See for yourself. Run an Internet search on how to get out of a bad mood, and instantly scads of remedies pop up. My favorite? "Banish a Bad Mood in 15 Minutes." Right. Ironically, the advice was published in *REAL SIMPLE* magazine.[5] Moods—especially bad ones—while they may be real, are anything but simple.

My personal remedy for mood madness is to enter the Psalms. While they may not banish a bad mood in fifteen minutes, they do provide real comfort. Camped in the Psalms, I know I am not alone in my funk. Consider some emotions of David in the midst of some seriously bad moods:

> **Distress**: "In my distress I called to the LORD … my cry came before him, into his ears. … He reached down from on high and took hold of me" (Psalm 18:6, 16).
>
> **Anger, Abadonment**: "How long, O Lord? Will you forget me forever? How long will you hide your face from me? How long must I wrestle with my thoughts?" (Psalm 13:1-2).
>
> **Hope**: "I am still confident of this: I will see the goodness of the LORD in the land of the living. Wait for the LORD" (Psalm 27:13-14).
>
> **Joy**: "The LORD is my strength and my shield. My heart trusts in him and I am helped. My heart leaps for joy and I will give thanks to him in song" (Psalm 28:7).
>
> **Praise**: Psalm 145, David's psalm of perfect praise.

Even in hard times, David emerges victorious in praise; though I bet it took a lot longer than fifteen minutes.

The Psalms elicit the "butterfly effect" on my moods. The butterfly effect—based on the poetic and whimsical question of M.I.T. meteorologist Edward Lorenz—asks, "If a butterfly flaps its wings in Brazil, does it cause a tornado in Texas?"[6] Scientifically speaking, he was asking if a very small natural force applied over a period of time and space could produce a larger cumulative effect on the whole system. Meteorologically speaking, I can't say. I do know, however, that one small snippet from a Psalm has a ripple effect on my life. And a series of Psalms over the course of a week can cause change in the weather pattern of my foul mood.

So send in the butterfly wings of Psalms. The storms will come, but by allowing the wave of Psalms to wash over our lives, we can begin to detect nano-sized positive changes. Overtime, these changes will have a cumulative effect on those around us and on our very lives. So go ahead. Reflect the light. Enact the butterfly effect. You won't be disappointed.

WONDERCISE

Butterfly Buffet

Seeking serenity? Try an afternoon in the company of butterflies, those winged wonders of creation. That's right: afternoon. No rolling out of bed predawn to witness first-flight behavior of the birds. Butterflies are much more my style.

Because butterflies are cold blooded, they need the warmth of the sun to rev up their engines and they accomplish this through a behavior called basking or reflectance. Using their wings as heat shields of sorts, some butterflies can reflect the heat off their wings to warm up their bodies. When encountering a butterfly in this state, you will be able to observe the majesty of the wings, which lie open like the pages of a book.

Once warmed, the butterfly will need some sustenance. They fly in search of nectar—the sweet, sugary beverage which lies buried in nature's goblet of glory, the flower. Planting a butterfly garden stocked with floral species sought by butterflies is a great way to attract butterflies to your yard and provide a butterfly habitat, the likes of which are rapidly disappearing.

But, for the impatient, gardening-challenged butterfly watcher, there is another way: Serve up a slice of summer in the form of a "sipping bar." Using readily available fruits, you can provide a smorgasbord of sweetness and entice butterflies into your presence.

The optimum conditions for butterflying occur on a sunny day with no clouds in the sky and temperatures ranging from 70° to 90° F. On such a day, prepare to meet a butterfly.

Knapsack Needs:

- Variety of fruits
- A bushel of patience

1. Fruit preparation: Place small amounts of different fruits—a slice of watermelon, a chunk of overly ripe banana (or you can slice, freeze, then thaw bananas to render them juicier), a few sliced grapes, and an orange slice on a plate. Experiment with different fruits to see what works best in your area. Softer fruits—the juicier the better—are easier for the butterflies to sink their proboscis into. Since the fruit will dry out and need to be changed every few days, I like to use small amounts. Besides, you are feeding butterflies; a little goes a long way.

2. Select location: Choose a spot to set up your sipping bar—either in a place where you can view it from your window, or a bench in your garden. Don't despair if you are trapped in a cement jungle. On a patio, set the dish among an arrangement of potted flowers.

3. Wait in wonder. Ultimately and eventually your patience will be rewarded with a shimmer and shine of the ephemeral kind. If not today, then perhaps tomorrow a butterfly will flutter by.

Promise of Hope

"Arise, shine, for your light has come, and the Glory of the Lord rises upon you" (Isaiah 60:1).

9
BEE DIVINE

"A bee is a ray of divinity." -Virgil

Admired for centuries, honeybees have wowed us with their industry, community, and productivity. Bees can make the goods! The prized honey of bees earned the title of "food of the gods" from the ancient Greeks. Heavenly honey. The importance of honey over the centuries may surprise you. It permeated all facets of life—and death.

In ancient Egypt a marriage contract was based on it: "I take thee to wife ... and promise to deliver to thee yearly twelve jars of honey."[1] Mummification parlors dipped in it. Check out these instructions found in a Persian manuscript for making a mummy:

> Find a ruddy, red haired man and feed him till he is thirty years old on fruit; then drown him in a stone vessel which is filled with honey and drugs, and seal up the vessel. When it is opened after the lapse of one hundred and fifty years, the honey will have turned the body into a mummy.[2]

Although we can't be certain anyone ever tried this procedure, I found this tidbit of information to be the most creative use of honey.

In Bible times honey oozed value. Moses preached about the sweet stuff.

> He brought us to this place and gave us this land, a land flowing with milk and honey (Deuteronomy 26:9).

The word honey is found sixty times in the Bible, with twenty-one exact matches to the delicious phrase "milk and honey" referring to the Promised Land. A substance valuable enough to be shared with kings and military officials, honey was included in one of the first biblical gift baskets (Genesis 43:11). The short version of the story is this: Due to a severe famine in the land, Jacob's family faced starvation. Jacob wasn't wild about the possibility of losing another son. Yet, in order to receive more food, the brothers would have to produce Benjamin, Jacob's treasured, youngest son. So the desperate father said,

> If it must be, then do this: Put some of the best products of the land in your bags and take them down to the man as a gift-a little balm and a little honey …

Today honey is still found in gift baskets. It's also found in lip balms, energy bars, and throat lozenges. But perhaps the most popular usage is as a sweetener for foods. According to the U.S.D.A. 2010 annual honey report, we consumed a sticky 1.2 pounds of honey per person in 2008.

What of its maker, the hardworking honeybee, the dynamo that delivers the goods? The honeybee is equipped in remarkable ways to make honey—and is the only being on earth that can.

The humble honeybee was scientifically named for its ability to bear honey. Technically that is incorrect. Bees don't bear honey, they manufacture it. Who knew? Certainly not Carl Linnaeus, the "Father of Taxonomy." In 1758, Linnaeus named the honeybee *Apis mellifera*—literally, "bee honey bearer" (in Latin, *Apis* = "bee," *melli* = "honey," *ferre* = "to bear"). However, in 1761, after it was discovered that bees don't actually carry honey, but nectar, which they process into honey, Linnaeus tried to rectify the error of his ways. He sought to re-christen the bee *Apis mellifica* ("honey-making bee"), but the new name didn't fly. According to the ancient order of the rule-giving guys on the naming of life ("the rules of synonymy in zoological nomenclature," but how boring is that?) the first name bestowed on a creature has precedence. And so the bearing name stuck. Like honey.

This honey-making bee harvests quite a lot of nectar. Author Susan Brackney estimates that for every pound of honey, four pounds of nectar are required.[3] Through a series of complicated and specialized tasks coordinated by a colony of very organized bees, we reap the results in the form of delectable, delightful honey.

Three social classes comprise a colony of honey makers: the queen, the drones, and the workers. The queen is in a class by herself, the sole matriarch of the hive. To be crowned Queen Bee comes with the responsibilities of Royal Reproducer (a.k.a. egg laying machine). Each and every day, at the height of the season, the queen produces between 1500 and 2000 eggs. At the low end, that is 1.04 eggs every minute for twenty-

HONEYBEE

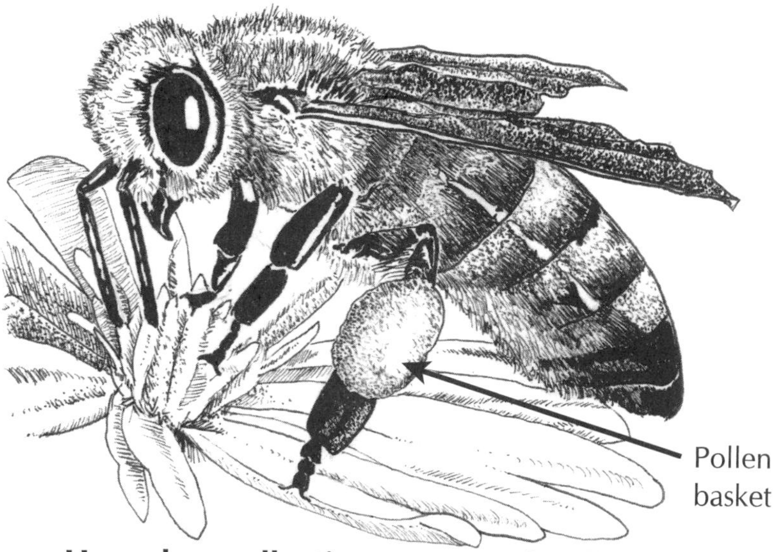

Honeybee collecting nectar and pollen

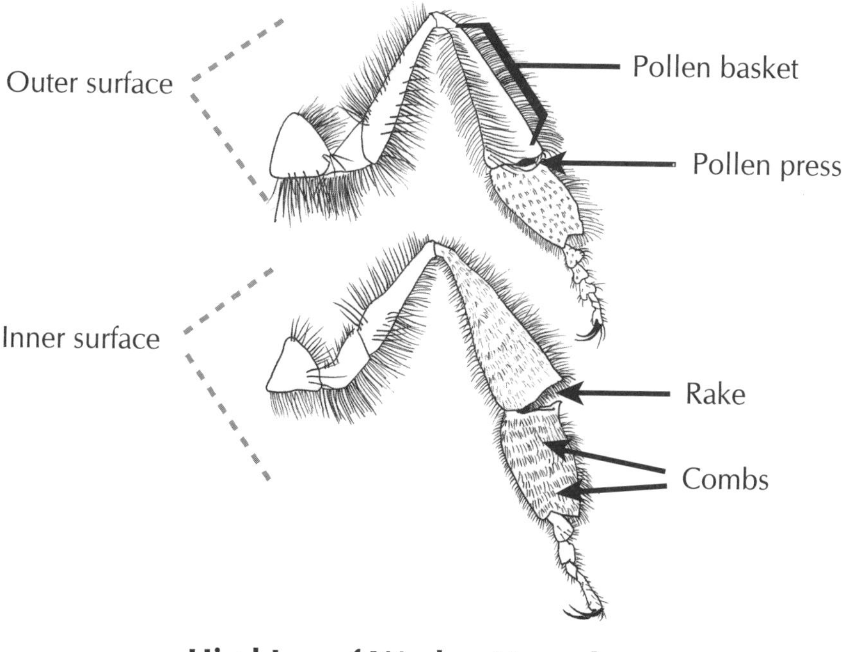

Hind Leg of Worker Honeybee

four hours with no potty or coffee breaks. Too busy to tend to self care like eating and hygiene, she leaves this matter to her attendants (worker bees). And I thought my life was busy! Perhaps being queen is not all it's buzzed up to be.

Then there are the drones—the male honeybees. Drones aren't going to make you green with envy either. They are defenseless, stingless and helpless. They can't even feed themselves. Their sole purpose in life is to mate with the queen. Then they die.

What's the other option? The lowly worker bee. These female bees comprise the bulk of the colony and have the longest honey-do list, hence the name "workers." It's a good thing, for the bee's sake, that there is a division of labor. Occupations and duties vary with age. A help wanted ad in the *Honeybee Gazette* might read like this:

Immediate openings in the following fields:

- *Construction worker*
- *Nurse*
- *Housecleaner*
- *Air cooler/dehydrator*
- *Chef*
- *Floral forager*
- *Directional dancer*
- *Security guard*
- *Embalmer*

Must be hard-working, fearless, and proficient at multi-tasking. Only team players need apply. Proof of age required.

Hive jobs are specialized, performed at certain stages and ages in a bee's life. For instance, jobs for the youngsters (as early as one day old) are hive cleaning, babysitting (the care and feeding of larvae) and queen tending. Middle-aged bees (we're talking weeks here—two to three for summer populations; eight to ten for winter populations) are more likely to engage in food handling (receive nectar), pollen packing, and comb building. After they have demonstrated a level of independence and responsibility, they qualify for jobs outside the hive such as ventilating, guarding and floral foraging.

While the job list is long, the workers are many (a healthy hive can host upwards of sixty thousand bees, with worker bees comprising the majority of the colony). A worker bee need not feel unprepared for the task at wing. She is remarkably equipped to do the job. All of the jobs. Over the course of a lifetime (the length of which varies seasonally from a 26.5 day average in the summer to 140 days in winter) the worker bee can and will do all of the above tasks.

Worker bees possess a variety of tools in their tool belt to aid them in their varied tasks. Let's explore some of that specialized equipment.

CONSTRUCTION TOOLS

Now this comb of a home is no slacker's shack—its construction is more elaborate than the Taj Mahal. Literally, the comb is an architectural wonder. In *The Biology of the Honeybee*, Mark Winston calls the comb "one of the marvels of animal architecture," and describes it in great detail:

> The precision and strength of the newly built comb is remarkable. For example, cell wall thickness is 0.073 mm, the angle between adjacent cell walls is an exact 120°, and each comb is generally constructed 0.95 cm from its neighbor…[4]

Even the precise thirteen degree angle at which the comb cell sits is important: the upward tilt prevents the honey from dripping out of the horizontal honeycomb.

And to think that it all starts with a wad of wax that Bessie Bee chews like cud. That's right. The medium for the comb is wax, which the bee manufactures from a set of wee wax glands embedded on the underside of its abdomen. Droplets of wax exude in liquid form, then solidify into small scales, which the bee tucks into a back pocket till needed.

When building begins, the bee grabs the wax scale from its pocket, pops it into its mouth and chews it like a wad of gum, until it is just the right soft and sticky consistency to begin comb construction. To understand the absolute absurdity of this remarkable feat, imagine if you were to build a shelter of sorts. Your material of choice: Double Bubble bubble gum. You chew, mold, and arrange each piece of gum into a shelter greater than fifty times your size and one hundred times your weight, constructed of hundreds upon hundreds of perfectly angled hexagonal cells. And you do this in complete darkness, with no computer generated measurements. Go ahead, try it. I can only imagine the sticky glob of goo from any feeble attempt I may try. I can't even draw a straight line, let alone build a wax house.

Admittedly, bees put my "close enough" style of carpentry skills to shame. Exactly how they perform such precise architectural measurements and tasks remains a mystery, but researchers have discovered an unbelievable tool the bee uses to maintain vertical orientation: hair plates—the bee version of the ancient plumb bob. Hair plates contain tiny hairs and are positioned at the base of the bee's neck. They work like a carpenter's plumb bob, telling the bee which way is up based on the air pressure exerted on these hairs. These hairs also enable the bee to maintain balance.

The amount of detail required to build a honeycomb sets my cells (brain cells) a bit off kilter. The math alone would require a degree in engineering. To say it is mind boggling is an understatement. Murray Hoyt, author of *The World of Bees*, found it a bit incredulous as well:

> It is completely incredible that, with thousands of bees coming up and adding their bit of wax to the spot where the 'drawing out' is going on, you don't get a thousand different variations of shape and thickness. You're led to the conclusion that every one of these thousands of insects in her own right must be a trained engineer.[5]

But it's not only the bee's engineering skills that dazzle; check out her dancing moves.

THE BEE DANCE

To find the goods, bees must dance. Seriously. Bees know and perform three basic dances: jitterbug, square, and ballroom. Or in bee speak, the round, the waggle, and the dorsoventral abdominal vibrating dance (this conjures up some great visual images in my mind). The dance moves communicate valuable information about the distance, direction, and quality of the food sources available to the troops.

Using the language of the dance, bees send out signals of sound and air emitted through wing and abdominal vibrations. The job of decoding the vibes falls to the receiving bee's trusty antennae, which are jam packed with a variety of special sensors. One such sensor is the Johnston's organ, which contains a whopping one-thousand ciliated sensory neurons. This tiny receiving device interprets the vibrations and provides the food scout with detailed directions to the food source. Once the bee knows the way, it flies off to get dinner.

COLLECTING THE GOODS

The main diet of honeybees are the floral products of nectar and pollen. Nectar is obtained from the flower via a specialized straw of sorts (the proboscis). This tool allows the bee to draw up the deliciousness out of the flower and transfer it to its honey stomach—sort of a Camelbak for bees. Back at the hive, the bee deposits the nectar into individual honeycomb cells. Fresh nectar contains up to eighty percent moisture, yet the finished product of honey has about seventeen percent moisture due to the worker bees' Annual Fanning Convention: bees rapidly beat their wings in unison effectively evaporating water from the nectar, and cooling the hive on a hot summer day. Bees then mix in a special brew of enzymes which transforms the product into honey. That's the liquid end of the deal.

The transportation of dry goods involves pollen and legs. Lots of leg. With some serious stubble issues. But that stubble has a purpose. Bee legs are equipped with tools to collect and stash the pollen as bees navigate the skies to bring home the bacon—or pollen.

For a moment, let's get past all the bristles and hairs of the bee leg. Shave them from your insect-repulsed mind so that we can explore this extremity in an open-minded, hairless sort of way and discover the magic of the leg. Bee legs are crucial to the life of the hive. Without the legs, pollen would have nowhere to hide … or ride.

The honeybee has three pairs of segmented legs. But the hind legs are highly specialized for pollen transport. Three nifty structures assist the bee with this task.

You may have noticed the pollen basket—that round nugget of gold on the hind leg of a bee evident after it has been in the presence of flowers. The structure of the basket itself is a smooth, concave depression on the outer surface of the hind leg. The basket is trimmed in a fringe of long curled hairs, from which one central bristle emerges to anchor the pollen. Rakes and combs are bristles on the inner surface of the hind legs and they maneuver the pollen into the pollen press, which packs the pollen into tight bundles, like pressing brown sugar on a spoon, and then the energy source is ready for transport. That is the wonder of the hind leg. Bees are endowed and gifted to survive and even thrive in their busy world. Barring no unforeseen circumstances, disease or predator mishap, the colony grows.

Eventually a healthy hive becomes overpopulated. Every comb cell is full. No room in the inn. Or hive. Time to invest in that second home. The real estate hunt begins. Call in the scout bees. After a series of inquiries, the new home is eventually selected and

> a third of the workers stay at home and rear a new queen, while the other two thirds of the workforce—a group of some ten thousand—rushes off with the old queen to create a daughter colony.[6]

Bees become so focused on the queen in transit, they follow her every move. Literally. If the queen, say, stops for directions, or a flight break, the whole caravan of followers (ten thousand bees, collectively beating their forty thousand vibrating wings) comes to a screeching halt. They are that tuned in to following their leader.

This scenario brings to mind the biblical story of Deborah. Deborah (quite literally the bee of the Bible; in Hebrew, her name means "bee") was the "royal decider" of Israel around 1200 B.C. Judge Deborah. Catchy name for a TV series, eh? But instead of deciding which issues are ripe for TV audiences, Deborah decided issues of the day to maintain justice in a corrupt land. Deborah was appointed to this political seat to liberate, deliver, and rescue the Israelites. Okay, maybe it could make for some great television drama.

Refresh your memory and read Judges chapter 4. When we meet Deborah, the Israelites were in a bit of a bind. Having lived by their own fleshly ways, God had "sold them into the hands of Jabin," the evil king of the land of Hazor. Deborah, being the woman of God that she was, longed to restore the Israelites to a right relationship with God, from whom they had turned away.

Problem was, Jabin possessed some serious hardware in the form of iron chariots—more metal than the Israelites could even hope to own. They could, however, fight back with a God of steel that Deborah hoped to reintroduce them to. Deborah had a plan. She summoned the military man Barak and told him the good news.

> Barak, the Lord commands you: 'Go, take with you ten thousand men (ironically the same number of bees in a colony that depart the comfort of the hive to seek new territory) and lead the way to Mount Tabor (site of huge battle).'

Can't you just hear him quaking in his boots? Barak, the "worker bee" who feared moving forward without the royal decider, responded,

> If you go with me, Queen Bee (my addition) I will go; but if you don't go with me, I won't go.

Sounds just like the buzz bees make when their queen stops to rest on their journey.

Barak's words make me smile: "If you go, I'll go, but if not, just forget it" (my translation). I love his honesty. And I can relate to his fear. It is scary to face demons on our own. In the end, Deborah (and ten-thousand men) decided to ride along. And true to Deborah fashion, she made it clear Barak would suffer the consequences for taking the "chicken" way out. Nonetheless, the Israelites succeeded and were victorious in battle and they enjoyed peace for forty years.

How do we face the battles of our daily lives? When the Lord commands, do we go? Or do we list excuses? I'm too tired. Too busy. Or are we just plain stubborn and self-willed? Oh that I would respond as a worker bee, who works with every gift it has been given and strives to bring success to the hive at all costs.

God gives us exactly what we need for what he calls us to do. So what are you waiting for? Sip from the sweet power source of the master. And transform your nectar-filled spiritual life into honey. It's golden.

WONDERCISE

Operation Bee Watch

Spend some time in the presence of bees in their natural environment. With over four thousand species of native bees in the United States, you may find the imported honeybee sipping nectar with other flower-loving bees. Some possibilities are the fuzzy black and yellow bumble bee, the small, shiny metallic green sweat bee (named for its attraction to the salty stuff), or even a large carpenter bee (named for its habit of boring into and nesting in wood).

Knapsack Needs:

- Hand Lens
- Field guide to insects

Find a park, garden, or nursery-any place where flowers are in bloom. Visit at several different times of the day: early morning, noon, and early evening. While you are patiently waiting for bees, observe a few different flowers with your hand lens. When a bee arrives, pay attention to the bee's behavior and ask yourself these questions:

1. What type of flower attracts honeybees? Note its shape, color, and size.
2. Where does the bee touch down on the flower?
3. What does the bee do when she lands?
4. How long does she stay?

If you can keep an eye on the same bee, notice how many flowers it visits. Note these observations in your notebook.

After observing its behavior, sit in contemplation. Enjoy the bee—in all its glory. And consider some wisdom from the early American bee keeper John Hunter:

> When studying with awe the wonders of the Bee-hive, so beautiful in

> their simplicity, so perfect in their ends, can we fail to acknowledge the presence of that All-guiding Hand, who, by these little insects and all their wondrous works, teaches man a lesson of industry, forethought, and order.[7]

Amen!

Promise of Hope

"For we are God's workmanship, created in Christ Jesus to do good works, which God prepared in advance for us to do" (Ephesians 2:10).

10
HUMMINGBIRDS
A Lesson in Balance

"Life is like riding a bicycle—in order to keep your balance, you must keep moving." -Albert Einstein

I have a tendency to ride life like a bicycle. In an endless cycle of movement I pedal towards success in all I do. I want to be a great wife and mother, excel as a biology research technician, maintain an immaculate house (and my sanity) and write a book—all at the same time. This works for a while. A very short while. Then I crash.

What went wrong? I lost my balance. Crucial to a smoother (notice I did not say smooth) "cruiser" life is a delicate balance of work and rest. To maintain balance, I depend on a daily tune-up session with the master technician himself.

We see this in the familiar Bible story of Mary and Martha, sisters of stillness and sizzle, who respond to Jesus in their midst in vastly different ways. We will unwrap that story in a moment. But first let's look out the window. Nature has what I call a "Marymartha" bird. At least that's what I would have named the hummingbird whose daily rhythms of life alternate between periods of extreme energy expenditure and extreme stillness. Let's sit with a hummingbird a spell and observe a life lived in balance.

Hummingbirds captivate and fascinate. Perhaps it is because of their size: the very name of the hummingbird family Trochilidae is from the Greek word *trochilos*, meaning "small bird." The smallest bird known is the bee hummingbird, weighing in at 0.07 ounces, less than the weight of two thin dimes. Another part of our fascination with these birds is their speed. With the fastest wing beat (two thousand revolutions/minute) and heartbeat (1200+ beats per minute) of any bird, hummingbirds zip through the sky's express lane.

While hummingbirds are admired for their petite size and speedy moves, I hunger for their metabolism. Hummingbirds need a metabolic rate that moves at the speed of light (or so it seems) to pay for their high energy lifestyle. Known to consume twice their weight in nectar each day, hummingbirds eat as if their life depends on it. And it does.

The average hummingbird weighs about a tenth of an ounce, or slightly less than the weight of a nickel, and their required ten calories a day seem miniscule. But if I were to re-calibrate those numbers for my weight and daily caloric requirement, that number would astound you. It astounds me.

Let's do the math: I weigh 150 pounds. At sixteen ounces per pound, I weigh a whopping 2400 ounces (no wonder I prefer to hear my weight in pounds, not ounces). Translated into a hummingbird metabolism, I would need ten calories for every tenth (.10) of an ounce I weigh. In order to maintain my current weight, I would require—drum roll, please!—240,000 calories a day. That, my friends, is a ridiculously high metabolism.

This is a high energy bird, requiring a ridiculously large calorie intake. How they accomplish this feat is remarkable. Nectar is not only the food of the gods, but it is also the primary source of nutrients for hummingbirds. And they have the means to access it.

The trick is in the tongue. For years, the widely accepted belief was that the hummingbird used its tongue as a straw, sipping its floral beverage. Until recently. Using high-speed video cameras and transparent feeders, researchers at the University of Connecticut were able to peer inside the secret world of hummingbird tongues. What they found is astonishing. The hummingbird tongue resembles a "two-tined fork" fringed with tiny hairs. When the tongue comes into contact with that liquid gold, these hairs curl inward as a ribbon does to the scrape of scissors, effectively trapping the fluid and transporting it into its mouth.[1] Makes my tongue curl in sweet anticipation just thinking of it.

Just as man does not live on bread alone, so the marvelous hummer does not solely exist on sweet sugar solution. Throw in a bug or two for good measure and protein. That's right. Bugs. If their specially-fashioned, nectar-trapping tongue amazed you, wait till you get a load of their beak-tweaking behavior. Using a process called "hawking," hummingbirds can grab an insect on the wing. Anyone who has tried to swat a mosquito knows the difficulty in this task. For hummingbirds, it's a snap. Literally. With snap action beaks, they grab grub on the go.

According to researcher Gregor Yanega of the National Evolutionary Synthesis Center,

> Hummingbirds need the equivalent of three hundred fruit flies a day to survive.[2]

Makes my jaw ache just thinking of it. But the hummingbird can snag a bug with a tweak of its beak in less than a hundredth of a second. Seems its lower beak is "stiff yet springy, like a diving board," allowing it to flex as much as twenty-five degrees when opening.[3] Ever try to catch a fly ball with your mitt closed? Open the mitt, and the ball has a better chance of hitting the target. By flexing its lower beak, the bird now has a larger surface area with which to land its lunch.

So hummingbirds are nectar-trapping, speedy-snapping aerial acrobats. Fast food wonders of the ornithology world, hummingbirds work to collect the calories necessary to support their high energy lifestyle. And because hummers eat on the fly—they don't perch at the bluebell bar, they literally use the fly through. This requires precise movements. Hummingbirds can fly up, down, backwards, and even upside down—just as amazing is its ability to hover.

Let's park it in the hover mode. The hummingbird stiff-wings its way into a hover. Looking at the bone structure, you can see that the wing of a hummingbird is built of a long "hand" and short upper and lower arm and can only move its wing at the shoulder joint. The wing is a stiff blade, much like that of a helicopter rotor blade. Also like a helicopter is the hummingbird's ability to hold its body perfectly still while rotating its wings rapidly in figure eight motions, made possible by the ball and socket joint arrangement at the shoulder.

Hummingbirds are a study in incessant movement and energy expenditure. But even hummingbirds must rest. You might wish for the ability to "noctivate" too.

Excuse me? Come again?

Read on …

Hummingbirds are warm blooded animals, yet due to their small body size and lack of down "comforter" feathers, if they shut off their metabolic "engines," they will likely have trouble maintaining body temperature. So what happens when the sun goes down, flowers close up shop and hummers need to catch some shut-eye?

An "idling speed" would help them survive the night. So God

HUMMINGBIRD

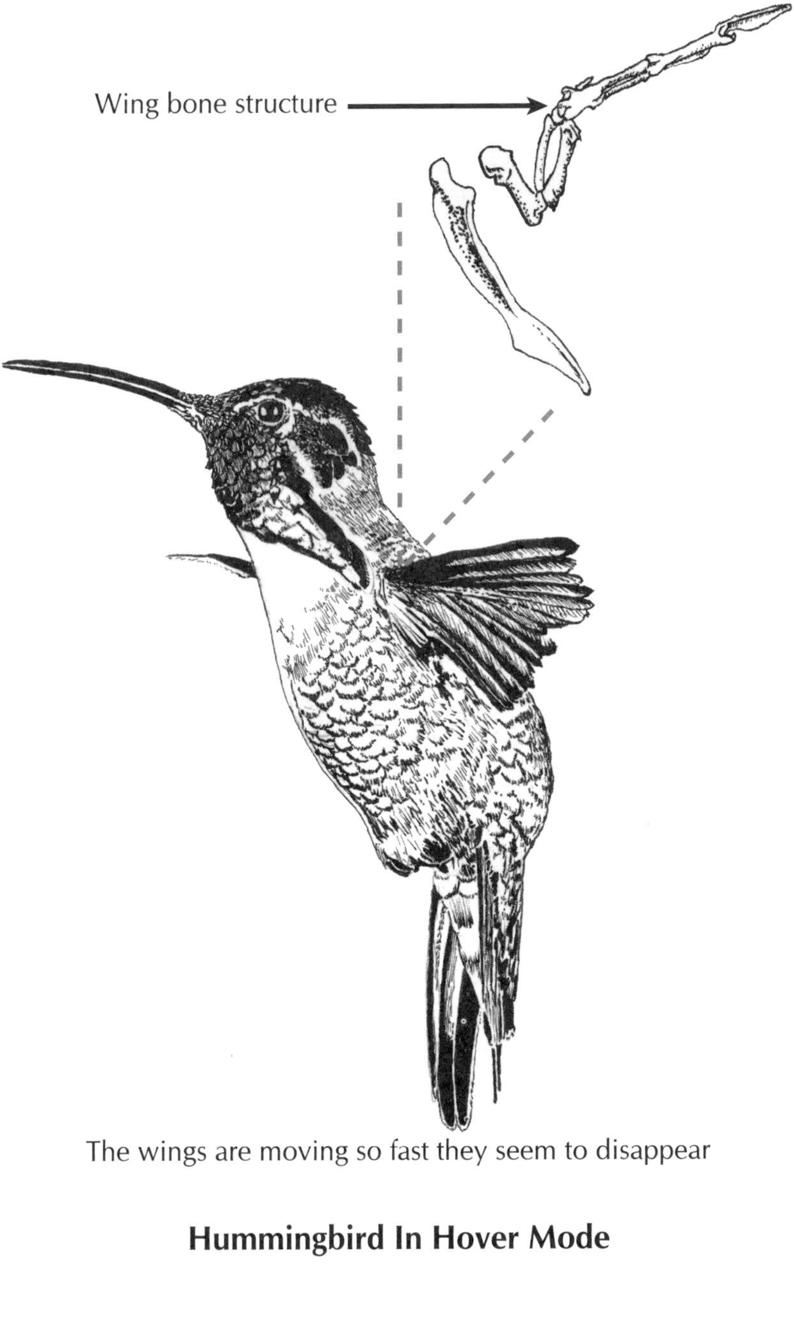
Wing bone structure
The wings are moving so fast they seem to disappear

Hummingbird In Hover Mode

invented torpor.

Torpor is sort of a "one-night-stand" hibernation—which proper scientists call noctivation. Hummingbirds—and also a few other birds and small mammals—have the ability to turn down the dial on their racing heartbeat overnight, from 1220 beats per minute to 60 beats per minute, thereby lowering their metabolic rate by as much as 90%. In this diminished energy state, the hummingbird can also drop its body temperature-from its daytime norm of 104°F to 40°F.

In the state of torpor, the hummingbird is a master of energy conservation—using up to fifty times less energy overnight than when going about its normal daily activities. The hummingbird has the innate ability to still itself for the purpose of restoration and conservation. Those of us unfeathered "energizer humans," who rarely stop to eat or sleep, would do well to follow suit.

The importance of balance in our daily lives is illustrated in the biblical story of high energy Martha and the more torpid Mary (Luke 10:38). Jesus has arrived in their home. I wonder if he called ahead. The way Martha is huffing and puffing, I doubt it. Martha flies about in a frenzy of preparation, her hummingbird tongue-like fingers licking their way around the kitchen, seeking to prepare a meal for unexpected guests. Grinding the flour, lighting the fire, drawing the water … it's not like she can pull frozen lasagna out of the freezer. No wonder her beak was out of joint.

Then there was Mary. A study in stillness, resting at Jesus feet. Absorbing his life-giving words. Mary was engaged in refreshing her stores of energy with the words of the Master.

All at once, the negatively charged energy of Martha bursts into the room and splits the stillness. Martha spits anger and frustration:

> Lord, don't you care that my sister has left me to do all the work by myself? (Luke 10:40).

Piercing the tension, Jesus speaks:

> Martha, Martha, you are worried and upset about many things, but only one thing is needed. Mary has chosen what is better, and it will not be taken from her (Luke 10:41-42).

Got that? Mary has chosen what is *better*. Jesus does not say that you should leave the cares behind and sit in stillness at his feet. He says to balance your daily duties with him, his Word.

> Seek first his kingdom and his righteousness, and all these things will be given to you as well (Matthew 6:33).

The hummingbird is built for both worlds: being and doing, resting and working. We would do well to emulate that behavior. Jesus commands it. I, for one, am going to still my wings each morning and take time to sit at Jesus's feet before rising to serve. I need the restorative presence of the Master to survive.

Care to join me in a time of torpor?

WONDERCISE

Hovering Hummers

Bring some hummers to your own backyard. Make your own hummingbird brew from sugar and water. It's easy and inexpensive to make. Another way is to plant natural hummingbird attractors—flowers such as honeysuckle, trumpet vine, fuchsia, and bee balm. Different syrups for different folks. Either way, prepare to sit back and observe the masters of balance—hummingbirds at work and rest.

Knapsack Needs:

- 1 cup white granulated sugar
- 4 cups water
- Hummingbird feeder

Mix sugar and water in a pan. Heat on stove until mixture reaches a boil, and then remove from heat. Stir until all of the sugar is dissolved. Cover and cool. Fill your feeder according to manufacturer's directions. Choose a quiet location outside. I like to place mine in view from my kitchen window, so I can enjoy their antics throughout the day.

Each time I pass by the feeder, it serves as a reminder to maintain balance in my life—and to allow myself times of "torpor." Those are the precious moments where I simply sit with God. That's refreshment.

Promise of Hope

"Be still, and know that I am God" (Psalm 46:10).

PART III
Gifts of the Deep

"If there is magic on this planet, it is contained in water." –Loren Eiseley

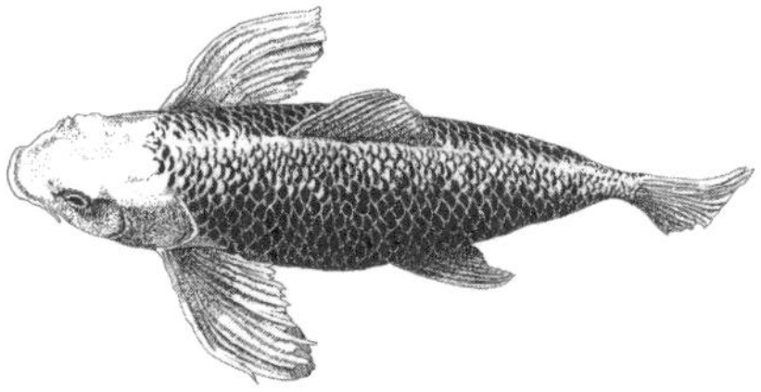
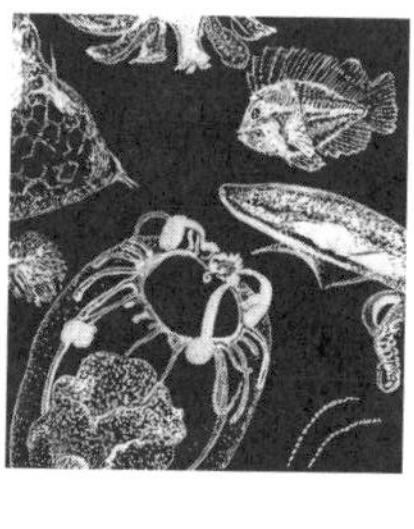

11

DANCE of the SAND DOLLAR

"Praise the Lord; praise God our Saviour! For each day he carries us in his arms" (Psalm 68:19, NLT).

My friend Pam worships like a toddler. And that's a good thing. Here's why: When she lifts her arms in worship, she's asking God to pick her up—in much the same way a small child signals the need to be carried. And God, being God, stoops down to pick her up. When we are weary, God will carry us. Recently I was reminded of this by a sand dollar.

Walking on the beach one day, I spied a sand dollar. Not the typical sand dollar one normally encounters on the beach—bleached and deceased—but alive. Each spine spun a pirouette of purple. Yet this was no ballet; this was a solemn march. As I studied the stranded speck of sand dollar, it appeared as if each spine painstakingly reached towards the sea. I contemplated the biology of this creature as well as the biology of movement in my spiritual life.

Sand dollars and their relatives—urchins and starfish—are prickly spiny folks (classified as *echinoids,* a word hailing from Latin, "like a hedgehog"). And how! Sand dollars, in their living state, are dressed in a fine coat of velvet spines. This jacket is not just for looks. It has purpose. A sand dollar's spines play a role in both prey capture and locomotion. You read that right—locomotion. Sand dollars move. As if on a small conveyor belt of sorts, the sand dollar is propelled by hundreds of densely packed short-haired spines, which spin in a symphony of movement. What I find interesting is the range of motion sand dollars exhibit: they can move forward, backward or spin in circles, all while lying down.

One species of sand dollar, though, is a stand out and stand-up guy, literally. The Pacific sand dollar, *Dendraster excentricus*, is able to pull itself up into an upright posture. By driving an edge into the sand, the Pacific

THE PACIFIC SAND DOLLAR
(Dendraster excentricus)

sand dollar stands in an inclined position, as dishes stacked in a drying rack. In this position, the sand dollar can eat while standing up (we humans tend to frown on this practice), snagging choice morsels from the watery soup of plankton. This works swimmingly in calm waters; in rough waters, not so much.

When they can't avoid harsh seas, sand dollars have adopted the ostrich-like behavior of burying their heads in the sand. They dig in and go low. Great advice for all of us in tough times. Despite such evasive measures, sometimes a sand dollar is caught off guard by a rogue wave and is tossed ashore, even flipped upside down onto its convex top. This calls for drastic righting measures, for if a sand dollar cannot right itself, death is imminent. The act of righting can take several hours and is an arduous process.

In my own life, I find the ability to right myself when life's circumstances have turned my world upside down to be essential for survival. Sometimes the rogue waves of life take us by surprise, upend us and flip us headfirst on our faces. Believe me, when tossed into the land of spiritual wilderness, I would like nothing more than to continue to wallow in the sand. But to lie there is certain death—of a dream, a hope, a future. Sometimes, we just have to get up.

Life's upheavals are a common occurrence in the Bible as well. Consider the number of times God or his angels told people to "Get up!" When Gideon's army dwindled down.[1] When Elijah simply gave up.[2] And when Joseph lay down.[3] In each case, God commanded them to get up!

In certain seasons of life, the sand dollar too needs to get up and move out. Winter is a season of storms. Waves loom large. Seas roil. Rough seas can damage and even kill sand dollars. Wouldn't it be nice to be able to take preemptive measures and hightail it out of the danger zone? Sand dollars are gifted with just such an ability. Researchers have documented the sand dollar's ability to migrate.[4] And in 1998, researchers Cabanac and Himmelman discovered that sand dollars are capable of intentional directional movement.[5]

Research suggests that sand dollars move seaward in the fall and are shore bound in the spring. While exact reasons are unknown (the ability to converse with the sand dollar is not yet possible) it seems reasonable to assume that this movement correlates with seasonal storm and wave action. Winter brings fierce storms to coasts, so sand dollars migrate to deeper waters to avoid being battered by waves. With the arrival of spring, they move closer to shore, when threat of storm wave action has diminished. Could it be that sand dollars know to get out of a storm? A mind boggling thought.

Jesus warns us that in this life, storms will come and we had best not build our house on the sand, but on the rock. Sand dollars—being sand dollars—haven't read the Bible. And so they drive their solid skeletons into the sand as a way of life. But in a storm the sand can move, leaving sand dollars at the mercy of the sea. Perhaps that was the fate of the sand dollar I found on the beach. Rough waters can eject us from our comfort zones as well. Yet, God can use those storms to bring us closer to him.

Consider the life of John Newton, the famous composer of the all-time great hymn *Amazing Grace*. God used a life-threatening storm to transform Newton from a hardened, slave-trading sailor into a minister and hymn writer of renowned fame. Newton described the wretched condition of his pre-storm life:

> My daily life was a course of the most terrible blasphemy and profaneness. I don't believe that I have ever since met so daring a blasphemer as myself. Not content with common profanities and cursing, I daily invented new ones so that I was often strongly rebuked by the captain...[6]

When Jonah, er, John Newton confessed to the captain some of his bad choices, the captain exclaimed that "to his grief he had a Jonah on board."[7]

Storms changed everything. Over the next month the ship would be battered by a series of storms that would result in Newton's own lightning-bolt conversion experience. On March 10, 1748 the waves crashing onto the ship awakened Newton. Water flooded his cabin. Newton climbed topside, as angry seas stripped the sails and tore the timbers. In an act of desperation, Newton and his fellow sailors stuffed clothing and bedding to abate the flow of saltwater fountains that spouted through the damaged hull. The disaster turned Newton's thoughts heavenward.

> 'If this doesn't work, the Lord have mercy on us!' This (though spoken with little reflection) was the first desire I had breathed for mercy for many years.[8]

Newton recognized March 21 as his personal day of infamy.

> On that day, the Lord of heaven delivered me out of deep waters.[9]

He was delivered both literally and spiritually. Nearly four weeks after the storm began the battered ship delivered a changed man to shore. Though Newton's complete transformation was still years away, his journey back to God had begun. Back to God? That's right. In the beginning of his life, Newton's mother nourished him with a foundational faith. Sadly, at age seven, when Newton's mother died, it was as if God died too. Newton wandered away from all things religious. Later he regretted those AWOL years.

> It was my dear mother's hope that I would enter the ministry. Her death, and the life in which I afterward engaged, seemed to cut off that probability…[10]

Yet God delights in changing probabilities. He loves the long shot, the failure, and the "has been." God is in the business of restoration. God used Newton, sort of a Jonah-Saul combo, to create a world-renowned hymn.

Through the heartfelt words of the song, Newton pens his personal and painful journey—and the ultimate victory of God's amazing, saving grace:

> Through many dangers, toils and snares, I have already come…God has brought me safely home.

Author and Pastor Peter Rahme said of *Amazing Grace:*

> It is hummed and heard on every continent in this world. It transcends race, religion and even record categories.[11]

If Newton had not met God in the storm, perhaps we never would have heard Newton's name again. Yet his story is told some 250 years later and is immortalized in the famous hymn. God's power saves lives and rewrites history. God's power is the stuff on which legends are built.

The sand dollar, too, has earned a legend. The keyhole sand dollar (*Mellita quinquiesperforata*), whose name is based on its markings, has become symbolic of the life of Christ. On the top of its test, or skeleton, is a beautiful etching of a flower, at the center of which is a five-pointed star.

The flower image is said to represent the Easter lily. The star represents the brilliant light that guided the wisemen to Bethlehem. The five distinctive holes in its skeleton represent the four nail wounds and one spear wound that Christ suffered at the crucifixion. On the bottom of the sand dollar the delicate, etched pattern represents the Poinsettia, or Christmas flower.

But perhaps it is what is unseen inside the sand dollar that is the most compelling part of the legend: the "doves" as they are called, are white, porcelain-like calcium shards that resemble the wings of a dove. These represent the angels that sang to the shepherds on that first Christmas morning.

In a living sand dollar, these calcium "doves" are its jaws, a structure technically called Aristotle's lantern for its resemblance to a lamp used in Aristotle's day. These jaws are crucial in the nourishment of a sand dollar. In the legend, these porcelain-like "doves" represent the peace of Christ. Who is Christ, if he is not our peace?

> Peace I leave with you; my peace I give you. I do not give to you as the world gives. Do not let your hearts be troubles and do not be afraid (John 14:27).

His peace nourishes and sustains us.

So whether we are called to endure through the storm, or to get up after we have fallen, God calls us to move. When it's difficult. When we are tired. When we feel we cannot go on. In the face of defeat, we must push onward into his open arms. He will carry us. He bids us to come. And to change. Thank goodness, I am not who I will become, but thanks be to God, I am not who I was.

That's the power of locomotion—one spine at a time.

WONDERCISE

The Art of Beachcombing

The beach has always been a place of renewal for me. The beach is where I am "erased by today's tides of all yesterday's scribblings."[12] If you have the opportunity, go to the sea and experience the soothing rhythm of its tides. Observe God's marine wonders in their natural environment. Remember to capture the memory only with your mind or a camera; leave the creatures you encounter undisturbed. And use caution. Life on the northwest Oregon coast taught me that "sneaker waves" can catch you off guard and knock you off your feet—or at least soak your sneakers. Stay alert and check the weather, sea conditions, and tides before you go.

Knapsack Needs:

- Hand lens
- Camera (optional)
- Proper clothing (wear waterproof shoes, dress in layers)
- Hat, sunglasses, sunscreen

As you saunter along the shore, allow the wonder of the sea's treasures to tickle your senses. Hear the curled blue as it crashes ashore and delight in the graininess of sand between your toes. Allow the scent of salty sea air—God's aromatherapy—to permeate your being. Enjoy the ocean swell of wonder.

Promise of Hope

"In him, we live and move and have our being" (Acts 17:28).

12
NATURE'S SPARKLERS

"I will love the light for it shows me the way, yet I will endure the darkness because it shows me the stars."
–Og Mandino

I'm attracted to light like a moth to a flame. Have been since childhood. Not the esoteric, philosophical form of light. I wasn't that bright. I liked plain old light. Candle light. Star light. And bug light. I longed to bask in the glow of fireflies sparking the night sky. Just one problem. There wasn't a firefly for a thousand miles. Fireflies live east of the Rockies and I was on the West coast. Faced with geographical separation, I learned to live without them, but never lost my intrigue for firefly light.

One day, as a middle schooler, my hunger for firefly light was satiated in a most unexpected place. In the ocean. An evening field trip to the beach yielded glowing waves, which crashed onto shore with bursts of light. Nature's sparklers. I was awestruck. I encountered marine bioluminescence—produced by an overabundance of microscopic algae jumbled together causing the phenomenon we call "red tide."

Natural light produced by living organisms is called bioluminescence. The word itself literally means "living lights" from the Greek word *bios* for "living" and the Latin word *lumen* for "light." The appearance of bioluminescence is a truth stranger than fiction that plays like a mix of cartoon artistry with a spark of mad chemistry. Animal-produced light? Why? And how?

Light is essential for survival. We need it to see—both physically and spiritually. Physically, light is necessary to transmit images from the world through our eyes to our brains. And spiritually, we know that Jesus is light and that his Word lights our path. In much the same way, the natural light of bioluminescence provides light for survival in an otherwise dark world. For centuries, great minds pondered this wonder. Much of the world's bioluminescence exists under the sea. Let's dive into that light.

Two-thousand five-hundred years ago, Aristotle wrote of bioluminescence. He documented fish scales that were alive with liquid fire, noting even "the juice of cuttle-fish" shines with this mysterious light.[1] While Aristotle rather stoically described nature's living light, it was Pliny the Elder, a Roman statesman and naturalist, who added a touch of whimsy to the phenomenon. Pliny described a clam with glow lights

> to be glitter both in the mouth of persons masticating them and in their hands...[2]

My first thought is, *How did he know this*?

The clams in question were considered a delicacy in Rome. Now, let's have some fun. Imagine Pliny throwing a huge glow-in-the-dark Roman banquet. While eating hors d'oeuvres by candlelight (remember, no electricity back in the day) the men apparently chatted and laughed with their mouths open and full of seafood supreme. Pliny witnessed the wonder of bioluminescence—in a messy, manly, masticating kind of way—and shared this tasty tidbit of knowledge.

While Pliny spoke to the glittering gastronomic delights of bioluminescence, centuries later sailors discovered a practical use for this glowing light. During World War II, when faced with darkness on the great sea, Japanese soldiers would grab fistfuls of dried "sea fireflies"—crustaceans the size of tomato seeds. These creatures, when crushed and mixed with water, would emit enough light for sailors to read their maps.

Bioluminescence is a common oceanic occurrence. Scientists estimate that ninety percent of creatures suspended in salty seas are bioluminescent. However, living lights blink bright on dry ground as well, found in the likes of beetles and worms, fireflies and fungus for starters.

No matter if occurring on land or sea, the concept of animals or plants generating light is a bit of a baffler. Just how does this happen? Bioluminescence is a chemical reaction.

Now before you close your eyes and try to tiptoe away, wait. Prior experience teaching basic chemistry labs taught me that the words "chemical reaction" can elicit the bolt reflex. Please resist the urge. A chemical reaction occurs every time you mix a glass of chocolate milk, whip up a batch of cookie dough or fry an egg. A chemical reaction is simply this: two or more ingredients (of a molecular nature) come together and produce change.

Bioluminescence is a reaction that occurs when two chemicals collide to create light. Sounds simple, right? Not so simple is how the organism pulls it off. Unraveling the process has occupied researchers' minds since the 1600s. As the theory goes, organisms emit the ethereal glow when two naturally occurring ingredients—an enzyme called luciferin and its companion luciferase—combine for the shine. Do you hear the name Lucifer tucked in there? Does it ring any biblical bells? If it does, I wouldn't be surprised. The name occurs in the Bible: "O Lucifer, son of the morning" (Isaiah 14:12, KJV). And in 2 Corinthians 11 we find satan masquerading as an angel of light. The origin of the word lucifer is from the Latin: *lux* ("light") and *fer* ("to bear"). Yet there is nothing devilish about the luciferin here; it simply means "light bringer." And does it ever live up to its name. Here's how.

Bioluminescence works like the snap of those popular glow sticks. The light stick is a plastic tube that contains a smaller glass tube within it. In each separate tube are two different chemicals (luciferin/luciferase). When you bend the plastic stick, you snap the glass tube, causing those two chemicals to mix and *voilà!* you have created a chemical reaction that produces light. Bioluminescence in animals is the same kind of deal, without the glass tubes of course. The naturally occurring luciferase acts as sort of a matchmaker, bringing together luciferin and oxygen. Once united, sparks of light fly. Amazing.

This reaction differs from other light reactions, such as light of the sun, or the light of an incandescent bulb where the energy is released as heat. The bioluminescent reaction is referred to as cold light because no heat is produced. Quite comforting for the living organisms, I'm sure.

Whew. With the chemistry out of the way, let's look into the history of observing bioluminescence in the ocean. In 1876 the Challenger Expedition—sort of a Lewis and Clark adventure of the undersea world—launched. The ship travelled the world's oceans for four years and collected more than four thousand unknown species, many of those bioluminescent. One man on board found himself star struck. Research student Rudolph von Willemoes-Suhm described the glow of deep-sea fishes as they were pulled up from the abyss:

> When the trawl came up at night, [it] hung in the net like a shining star.[3]

Bioluminescence charmed another researcher, William Beebe, nearly a half century later. Beebe dreamed of pioneering into the deep. Beebe wanted to observe creatures in their natural environment below the sea. The collecting method at the time—dredging—reduced specimens to slimy goo after being brought to the surface. Beebe longed for a better way. So he designed and crafted (with the help of Otis Barton) an exploration device which allowed him to descend and observe the living lights in their own habitat. In 1930 Beebe achieved his dream. His successful journey under the sea was historic. Beebe became the first human to witness bioluminescence in situ, not quite twenty-thousand leagues under the sea, but an epic journey nonetheless.

While crammed in a small steel globe that dangled from a thick cable, Beebe witnessed the wonder of the undersea world and relayed his impressions via a phone line connected to the surface. Euphoric with excitement, Beebe tells of experiencing a

> tremendous wave of emotion, a real appreciation of what was momentarily almost superhuman, cosmic, the whole of the situation…[4]

That, my friends, is discovery at its finest: exploring new territory, and living to tell of it.

Though Beebe's dive occurred nearly seven decades ago, scientists are still sharing in the joy of discovery. In 2009, scientists combing the ocean depths with remotely-operated vehicles discovered a "Dr. Seussian" doozy: Green Bombers. Not quite *Green Eggs and Ham*—more like *Green Bombs and … wham!* This wild-water worm literally drops homemade bioluminescent bombs on unsuspecting predators. Defense strategy at its finest. Named *Swima bombiviridis*, this recently-discovered worm literally means "green bomber" (*viridis* is Latin for "green"). And *Swima*? *Swima* is an invented word, fashioned after the name of another marine worm named *Flota*. How cool is that? Love the creativity!

Karen Osborn, post-doctoral researcher at Scripps Institution of Oceanography says of the discovery:

> We found a whole new group of fairly large, extraordinary animals that we never knew anything about before.[5]

These animals were one to three inches; clearly perspective is everything.

Another Seussian marvel is the "one fish, two fish, bioluminescent blue fish" or as it is commonly called, the anglerfish (*Lophius piscatorius*).

BIOLUMINESCENT ORGANISMS

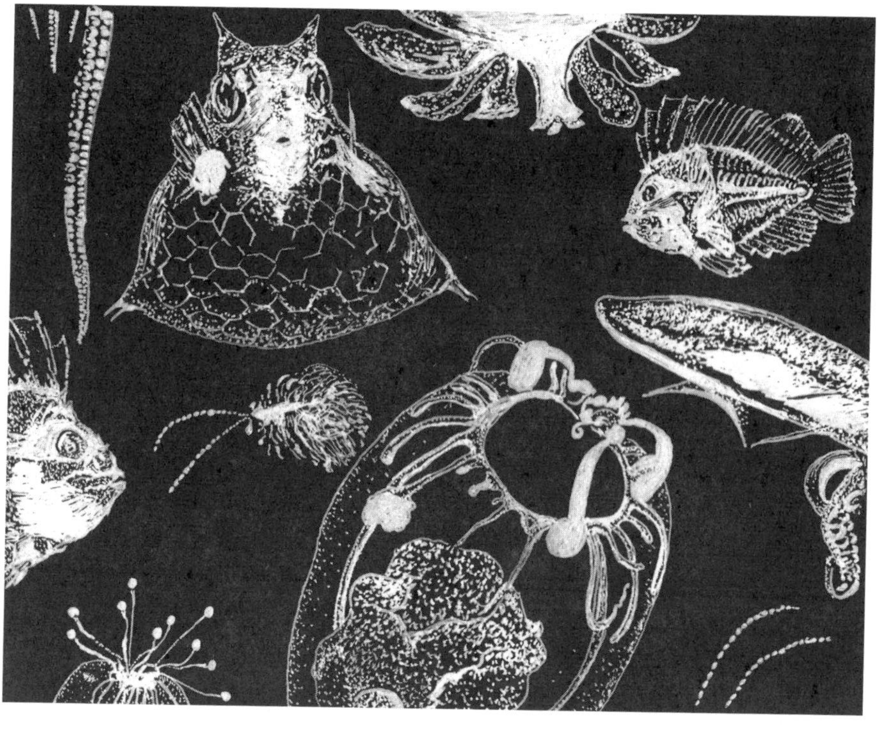

An Array Of Bioluminescent Organisms

This fish is one of two-hundred species that fish for a living. Seriously.

If you have ever gone fishing, most likely you have baited the hook. Anglerfish come equipped with a pre-baited hook in the form of a lighted lure. Living deep in the ocean, at depths where little to no light exists, the angler's glowing lure is a distinctive feature. The female sports this lure, complete with "fishing rod" (technically a modified dorsal spine) that grows directly out of her snout. Filled with millions of luminous bacteria, this "fisher-fish" innocently but deceptively dangles the lure over its ferocious-looking fanglike teeth.

The glowing orb attracts the attention of an unsuspecting hungry victim who swims in for a closer look—and snap! The anglerfish closes her toothed trap. I find this arrangement nothing short of miraculous. Couple this with the "green bomber" who manufactures and drops glowing bombs, and well, I'm awestruck by a creator who truly thinks of everything.

While we may be amazed by these stranger-than-fiction, light-producing wonders, each serves a purpose for the organism; the "green bombers" rely on bioluminescent "bombs" for self defense in the form of predator distraction. The angler fish utilize light to attract a meal. The "sea fireflies" referred to earlier are thought to flash blue for communication purposes. Scientists believe those to be the primary uses of bioluminescence—self-defense, attaining nourishment, and communication.

Remarkably, the same could be said of the light—the light of the Word—in our own lives. 2 Timothy 3:16-17 states,

> All Scripture is God-breathed and is useful for teaching, rebuking, correcting and training in righteousness, so that the man of God may be thoroughly equipped for every good work.

The Bible contains what I need. Problem is, sometimes I allow the turbulent waters of life to drown out the light. How can we overcome the darkness? How we can recapture the spirit of discovery in the Bible? Dive deep into the illuminating light of the word "Bible-luminescence."

Need the light of self-defense? Consider the words of Jesus, who fended off satan by quoting God's Word. Need nourishment? Read the Psalms, where references to God as light illuminate our lives and nourish a relationship with Creator God. Need direction? Open the Bible. It guides. We would do well to use God's light to direct our lives.

Bible-luminescence: It shines as naturally as the glow below the ocean.

WONDERCISE

Nature's Sparklers

On my bucket list is a visit to Bioluminescent Bay in Vieques, Puerto Rico. The bay's water is alive with 720,000 sparkling dinoflagellates in every gallon. That's a lot of bioluminescent bling.

If, like me, you can't get to Bioluminescent Bay anytime soon, roaming the sea's shore under the stars can add sparkle to life.

Knapsack Needs:

- Proper clothing (wear waterproof shoes, dress in layers)
- Flashlight
- Blanket

At certain times of the year, surface waters of the ocean are teeming with bioluminescent organisms that cause an electric blue glow in the water.

Occasionally you will be treated to the twinkle of flashing light in the waves. And pay attention to your feet as you walk along. As the pressure of your feet jostles the bioluminescent organisms below, sparks of light will pierce your footprints. Don't forget to lay a blanket on the bed of earth and immerse yourself in the wonder of starlight. Pure and simple. Recite Psalm 8 and revel in the wonder of God.

Promise of Hope

"The unfolding of your words gives light; it gives understanding to the simple" (Psalm 119:130).

13
FISH SCALE SCRAPBOOKS

"Adversity precedes growth."
-Rosemarie Rossetti

Snapshots soothe my soul. Especially treasured are snapshots of my children, droplets of their lives forever frozen in time. Sadly, the majority of my photos lie imprisoned in shoebox dungeons, only dreaming of acid-free paper and archival-quality books.

Oh, that I could be a fish. Fish carry scrapbooks neatly arranged on their backs, bellies, and tails, in the form of scales. Close examination of a fish scale reveals a fingerprint in a pattern of concentric rings. Written between these bands is the story of the fish's life, good times and bad.

Before we delve into the secrets of scales, let me just say that fish fascinate me with their "fishness," those characteristics that make them fish. Fish are armless, legless, water-bound creatures that possess the remarkable ability to live, move, and be under water. Could you survive under water? Not without assistance. Humans simply aren't made to be aquatic. Fish are. God has marvelously equipped them with an elaborate system of gills for extracting oxygen from its liquid form.

As a child, I remember trying to emulate a fish. I swam by wiggling my body, without arm or leg movement. I sank fast. Fish, however, sashay gracefully through the water using the undulating movement of their body. While suspended in water, fish contract their muscles alternately side to side to propel them through the water. Many fish have a streamlined shape which allows relatively rapid movement through the water. Their fins, often believed to function in locomotion, are actually directional in purpose. While the number and function varies with fish type, basically, the paired pectoral and median dorsal fin are key to directional changes, while the tail, or caudal fin, is responsible for propulsion. To enable vertical motion, fish possess a unique device called

FISH AND SCALES

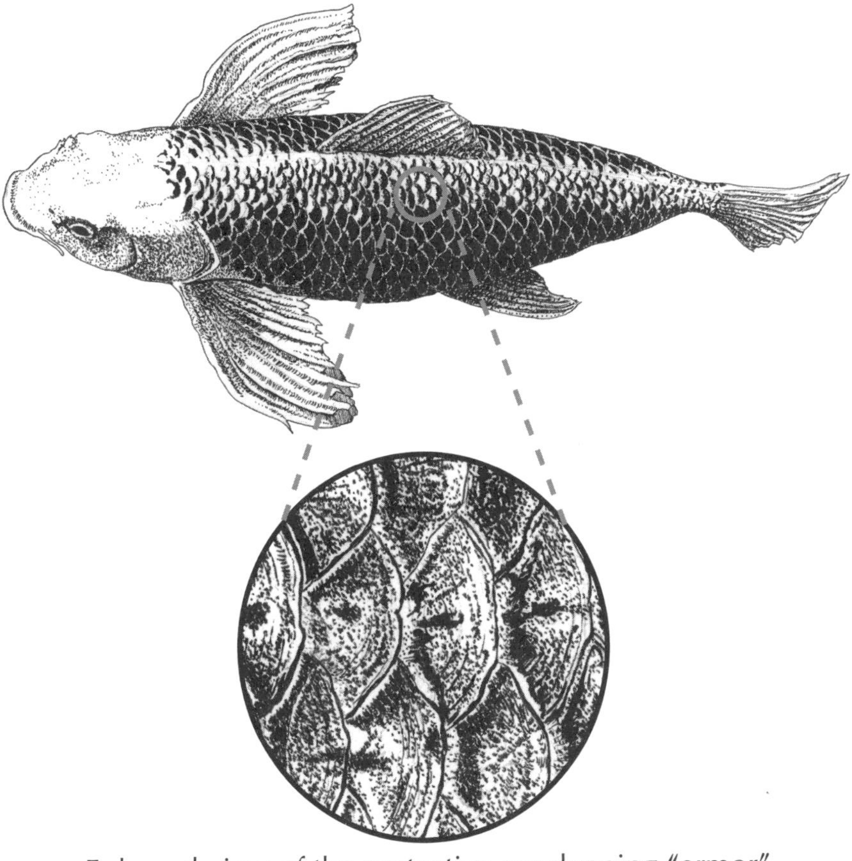

Enlarged view of the protective overlapping "armor" of the fish - its scales

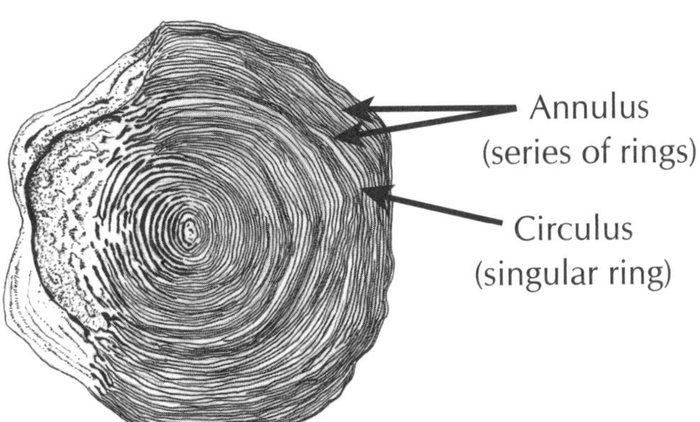

Diagram of an individual cycloid fish scale

an air bladder which they inflate to rise and deflate to dive. But I digress. Back to the wonder of scales.

What intrigues me about fish scales is that, like the annual rings seen in the cross section of a tree trunk, the rings of a fish scale represent years of growth. As a fish grows, each individual scale—the flexible, protective armor of a fish—adds lateral layers to keep the fish body covered. The phrase "I've got your back" takes on a whole new meaning.

Scales are a fascinating accessory in the world of fish fashion. Available in four basic styles—ganoid, placoid, cycloid, and ctenoid—fish scales fit a variety of body types. Ganoid scales are truly vintage wear, sported by the primitive, old-school fish: sturgeon and stickleback, gar and bichir. These smooth, diamond-shaped scales are reminiscent of a time when fish used armor plating to protect themselves.

Placoid scales are sported by sharks. Mimicking a Goth-style studded dog collar, these triangular scales have sharp pointed tips much like teeth. These scales are covered with enamel—the same stuff our chops are made of. An amazing creation, to be sure.

Cycloid scales cover the likes of trout, salmon, and herring, and could be considered casual wear of the clean cut guys. A fish appareled in cycloid scales, which are described as thin and smooth, reminds me of a fish in a well-worn pair of Levi's.

Lastly, ctenoid scales are the latest arrival to test the waters. These scales are similar in shape to cycloid scales but are accessorized with tiny, comb-like projections (ctenii) on their posterior edges (the edges that show). Perch and Bass are examples of fish adorned with ctenoid scales.

Cycloid and ctenoid are the two most common scale types in fish. These scales possess obvious growth rings. Biologists can estimate the age of fish using the annual growth rings on their scales, called annuli. Individual growth circles, called circuli, are added to the outer edge of the scale as the fish grows.

Scale growth rates vary with environmental conditions. Like detectives, biologists can infer much about a fish's living conditions from the growth patterns in their scales. Fish tend to grow more during warmer times due to greater food availability and have higher metabolic rates resulting in widely spaced rings. During cold winter months the days are shorter, causing fish to produce annuli that are closer together, depicted by narrow bands of rings.

In addition to food and light availability, disease and stress are also recorded on the scales. Good times, great growth. Bad times, little growth.

Our lives are also inscribed with growth rings. God desires to enlarge our lives, our territory, and our character. Significant events have left rings of differing widths surrounding our soul, forming our life's annuli. Spiritual progress occurs one ring at a time. However, unlike fish, our spiritual growth rings are inversely proportional to prime living conditions. The greatest growth occurs during the darkest times. Can we depend on ourselves during this time? Forget about it. It is precisely in rough waters, and when our resources are exhausted, that we cannot depend on ourselves.

That's when God steps in and sustains us. Note: I did not say this is pain free. The phrase "no pain, no gain" rings true. Growth occurs on the rim of risk. You risk failure, disappointment, loss. You gain growth. Occasionally, God has to nudge (okay, shove is more like it) us out of our comfort zones to enlarge our rings.

Take Peter, for example. A regular working class guy. A guy who loved to fish. Brutally honest and sometimes clueless. I can relate to Peter. In Peter, we find evidence of a person's life transformed by the touch of the Master's hand. Several stories in the Bible reveal a series of well-etched growth rings on Peter's life.

RING OF PURPOSE

Luke chapter 5 tells the story of Peter's career change—his life was about to be repurposed. Peter sailed on the Sea of Galilee making a living as a fisherman. I imagine that Peter might have been quite comfortable in his daily routine of casting nets and cleaning his catch. However, comfort zones do not produce growth in our lives. Jesus had other plans for this fisherman. Jesus called Peter to catch bigger fish, to become a fisher of men. This change in profession would require an entirely new set of skills. It was a stretch, but with his mentor Jesus, Peter left his nets and never looked back. Remember, though, that just before he left everything, he received Jesus' instruction: "Don't be afraid." Crucial advice. Growth can be an uncomfortable, scary stage in life. In taking steps to follow Jesus, Peter developed a giant growth ring, to be sure.

RING OF POTENTIAL

God met Peter where he was. God didn't wait until Peter attained perfection. He used him in his imperfect state, seeing his potential. Jesus tells Peter, "And I tell you that you are Peter and on this rock I will build my church" (Matthew 16:18). Commentaries tell us that the use of "rock" in verse 18 is a play on words. In Greek, *petros* means "Peter," which literally means "little rock," and the word "rock" in Greek is *petra*. The use of the two words can be interpreted as Peter (Petros) being the little rock on which the church, the massive rock (Petra), will be built. Jesus was telling Peter that he would become instrumental in the founding of the church.

The beauty of God is that he sees our potential—often before we see it ourselves. From the hotheaded, impulsive and roughhewn Peter, Jesus sculpted a masterpiece destined to become a pillar in the early church. And Peter, in his very human state, allowed himself to be inscribed by the Master. Jesus loves us not just for who we are, but who we will become. Thank God.

RING OF PERSPECTIVE

I am often a victim of my own faulty perspective. Peter, too, had perspective problems. At about three in the morning, while sailing the windy Sea of Galilee, Peter saw Jesus walking towards him on the water. Doubting his vision, Peter asked, "'Lord, if it is you, tell me to come to you on the water.' 'Come,' he said" (Matthew 14:28-29).

Peter defied his doubts, forgot his fears, and focused on Jesus. He stepped out of the boat onto the water and began to walk toward Jesus. But when he saw the wind, he was afraid and began to sink. Peter lost perspective. His focus drowned in a sea of fear. He cried out "Lord, save me!" (verse 30).

The compassionate and understanding Jesus immediately "reached out his hand and caught him" (verse 31). In this experience, Peter gained the solid growth ring of perspective and learned to stand firm in troubled times; to focus on Christ and not the problem at hand.

As with Peter's life, I can see specific times where growth emerged from a situation that God allowed in my life. Two things I have learned . First, God's growth plan is individualized and unpredictable. No assembly line spirituality here. God never grows two individuals the same way. He uses different techniques specialized for the uniqueness of who he created each of us to be. We are handcrafted one-of-a-kind works, each requiring a different instruction manual for operation. Second, God believes in spiritual growth spurts. Growth is an automatic process. It just happens.

Sometimes growth hits us like a tornado, other times it flows through us as a gentle breeze. The point is we don't control it. Not by our might, but by God's Spirit.

So consider your life to be God's fish hatchery. The fish farmer God is growing through your life experiences. Keep swimming. Against the current when it is difficult, or treading water when it's boring. Remember that you are living, breathing, and growing. Not bad, considering the alternative. Dead fish don't grow. They just stink.

WONDERCISE

Exploring Fish

FISH WATCH

While many of us would love the time and money to afford the luxury of a snorkeling trip in the tropics, observing fish can be as simple as a trip to the pet store.

Take time to see the fish. Notice the beauty of the rhythmic motion of its gills, as it pumps water through the gill flaps and bathes the gills with a fresh supply of oxygen to its blood. Observe the smooth scales that help it to glide ergonomically through the water. See God's fingerprints in the details of this creation. Contemplate the wonder of God.

EXTRA-ORDINARY WONDER: Fish Prints—Gyotaku[1]

Remember finger painting as a child? This is "fin" painting. Using the fins and body of the fish, we are creating art in a rubber stamp kind of way. Fish prining—gyotaku (*ghee-oh-tah-koo*) is believed to have originated in Japan in the early 1800s. Japanese anglers used it to record the size and species of their catch before selling or serving their treasures. Gyotaku later became a creative art form. Through the process of gyotaku we can learn to appreciate the beauty and intricacy of the fish.

Knapsack Needs:

- Fresh fish (bigger fish make better subjects)
- Newsprint paper (advance to traditional rice paper later)
- Water based ink or tempera paint
- 1" paint brush
- Cleaning supplies (paper towels, newspapers, salt)

METHOD:

1. Wash fish with water to remove its protective slimy layer (a gentle scrub with salt helps). Rinse. Pat dry.

2. Place fish on an old towel on your work surface. Using a brush,

apply a thin, solid layer of paint (or ink) over the fish. Use sparingly, or your print will be a glob of fish, lacking detail.

3. Place paper on top. Using your fingers, working from the center outward, rub the paper firmly to capture the shape and features of the fish's body. Be careful not to let the fish shift as you work.

4. Carefully remove the paper. Turn upright and let it dry. The result is the mirror image of your fish—a work of art. Note: If you aren't satisfied with your work, you can try again. Your prints will improve with practice.

5. Wash fish thoroughly, and prepare it for a meal. The old adage of "you catch it, you eat it"applies—after all, that's what the traditional gyotaku masters did.

As you reflect on this activity, remember the gift of the fish, the wonder of its unique characteristics, and celebrate the original artist—Creator God.

Promise of Hope

"He who began a good work in you will carry it on to completion until the day of Christ Jesus" (Philippians 1:6).

14

BARNACLES
Built for Adversity

"Cast your cares on God; that anchor holds."
–Frank Moore Colby

Perhaps you can swim like a fish, but can you cling like a barnacle?

The barnacle inhabits the inhospitable environment of the ocean's rocky shore. Yet it clings to the rock with such tenacity that it cannot be moved, even by crashing waves. How does the barnacle accomplish such an Herculean feat?

Good question. The barnacle, that common yet curious calcium-encrusted creature, has intrigued countless souls over the years. And captivated one man to the point of obsession. The famed Charles Darwin was so intrigued by the mystery of the barnacle that he devoted eight years of his life to unraveling the fascinating features of barnacle biology—from their shape-shifting larval forms to their ability to eat with their feet while standing on their heads. Darwin discovered barnacles to have

> variation beyond his wildest imaginings … no heads, stomachs, digestive systems, but with the largest penises proportionate to size in the animal kingdom. It was a brave new world.[1]

I'll say. But long before Darwin's quest to crack the code of barnacle anatomy, folklore spun tall tales of barnacle trees that birthed barnacle geese. Truly. As the story goes, the tree (actually, the stalks of the barnacle) sprouted buds (the baby barnacle) appearing as young birds dangling by their beaks over the water. At the proper time, the baby birds would drop into the water and develop into full-sized geese.

Perhaps that tall tale inspired Darwin to set the record straight.

BARNACLE

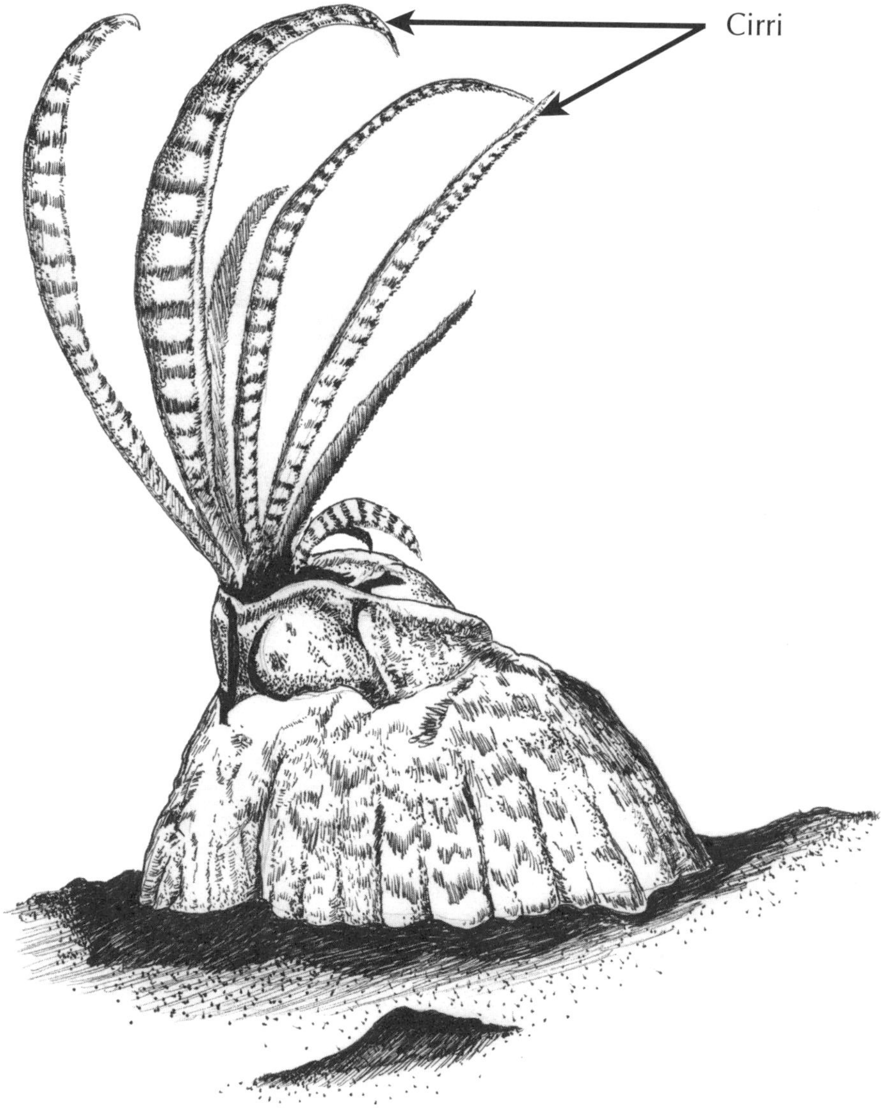

Adult Barnacle Feeding

Whatever his motives, Darwin's studies shed new light on barnacle biology. Darwin noted two types of barnacles: stalked (the tree type) and sessile—attached directly to the substrate with no stalk. In this chapter I deal only with the sessile barnacle.

A barnacle begins life as a microscopic squirt of a guy, floating on the mercy and whims of the current. The baby barnacle, called a nauplius larva, resembles something out of the science-fiction genre with its triangular teardrop body sporting one eye, two fuzzy antennae, and three pairs of legs. Several molts later, the larva transforms into the cypris stage, its new persona looking somewhat like a miniature bike helmet with legs.

The main objective of the cypris stage is to find a place to settle down. Operation exploration is of such importance that it doesn't even stop to eat. Crawling about, the cypris probes possible home sites with its sensory antennae. Helpful clues for a settling site are the pheromones (fancy animal-style perfumes) secreted by other barnacles. It's in the barnacle's best interest to settle near his own kind. This prevents isolation—a sure death sentence for the colonial lifestyle of this barnacle. Upon approach to the site, the barnacle pops out its "landing gear"antennae, performs its last (and permanent) headstand and settles, quite literally, for the rest of its adult life. Shell-ter-less and homeless, the barnacle begins the business of home construction—a cone of calcium carbonate complete with a trap door.

This trap door is necessary to survive the tidal flux of the day; twice in a twenty-four hour period the barnacle is exposed to the elements. During the dry times, the barnacle withdraws into its calcium-carbonate cave and closes the watertight hatch, a double set of French doors of sorts, with each half composed of a pair of interlocking, rock-hard calcium plates (terga and scuta) fitted neatly in the center of the cone. Here the barnacle bides its time until the waters return.

With the advance of the high tide, the barnacle breathes a sigh of relief. Muscles relax. The barnacle opens the doors to the watery world and unfolds its limber limbs. It's mealtime. Extending its flexible feathery forks, the barnacle prepares to grab a bite to eat. Barnacles are filter feeders, which means they strain their food from the water. Formally called cirripeds, from the Latin *cirrus* ("fringed") and *pedis* ("foot"), barnacles feed using their feet as sieve baskets, trapping small plankton for sustenance.

Admittedly, the barnacle's acrobatic performance of eating is extraordinary, yet researchers are investigating still other barnacle marvels—specifically their adhesive qualities. Seems researchers have a serious case of barnacle envy. Barnacles secrete Super Glue supreme, superior to any manmade adhesive. Finding a recipe for synthetic barnacle glue would revolutionize the world of dental and medical procedures.

At least one company, the Nerites Corporation, is working to find that recipe. Head chef (company president) Tom Mozer, says of the barnacle binder, "Here we have a glue that can stick to any surface and still work, even if it is dirty or wet."[2] Scientists hope to develop a synthetic version of nature's formula available for medical use in the next few years. Presently, Nerites has patented a prototype under the name Medhesive.

What we know about the natural sticky stuff is this: a barnacle can produce two types of glue—a temporary paste for the purpose of stability while the barnacle babe inspects its possible new digs; and a permanent stuck-to-you-forever glue. The barnacle keeps the temporary paste stored in an antennal segment. When a possible site is located, the barnacle antenna attaches as a "large thin sucking disc" to the site and secretes the sticky goo.

If the site passes muster, the barnacle then pulls out the big "glue guns" from behind its eyes and shoots out the tough stuff: permanent barnacle cement, recognized as "the most durable and toughest connection in the living aquatic world."[3] Like something out of a Dr. Seuss book, the barnacle sports a pair of kidney-shaped glands behind its compound eyes which manufacture the goods. And this is no ordinary Super Glue. The Office of Naval Research states that the barnacle

> secretes a rapid underwater-curing cement that is among the most powerful natural glues known-with a tensile strength of five thousand pounds per square inch.[4]

Five thousand pounds! Imagine a hippopotamus dangling by a steel cable anchored with a glob of barnacle bonder. The super sticky stuff holds true underwater and withstands temperatures of up to 440° F. Move over, Gorilla Glue, you may have met your match.

Actually, I could use a little dab of the durable stuff in my own life. I tend to lose my grip when things get chaotic. Yet I already have something—someone—that sticks stronger than barnacle glue. My God promises to never leave me, to hold me close, and to hold me tight—no matter what the situation. His bond will not fail.

King David, a man after my own heart, experienced times of severe slippage in his life. Yet, his desire was to cling to God. He knew when he needed a fix of the godly glue. Psalm 63 details a difficult time in David's life when things seemed to be coming undone. Driven from Jerusalem, David sought refuge in the desert of Judah to escape his rebellious son, who sought to kill him. Yet despite his dire circumstances, David knew the secret to prevent his world from falling apart. God Glue—a "glue" that holds.

If we explore Psalm 63, we see and feel David experiencing a low tide of his own, as he cries,

> O God, you are my God, earnestly I seek you; my soul thirsts for you, my body longs for you, in a dry and weary land where there is no water (verse 1).

Despite his despair, David is able to recall what he has seen in the past: the power and glory of God. He takes time to reflect on the truth that God is … and God can. Because of this, no matter what, David trusts.

And David praises. That's right, in the midst of the trial in the heat of the desert, David gives God praise.

> I will praise you as long as I live, and in your name I will lift up my hands (verse 4).

Thanksgiving produces a stress-relieving effect. Fear and praise cannot co-exist. David brings it home in verse 8, his resolve thoroughly set:

> My soul clings to you; your right hand upholds me.

Facing life challenges? Be like a barnacle. Hold tight during adversity with the supernatural Super Glue that comes only from the Rock that cannot move. Set your anchor upon the Rock. And cling.

WONDERCISE

Barnacles: Witness the Wonder

On your next trip to the tide pools, enjoy some time exploring the rocks of the intertidal zone, home to the barnacle. Remember, we are guests in their home—tread lightly and carefully for their sake and your own. And always face the ocean and be aware of the tides and waves.

Knapsack Needs:

- Hand lens
- Slip-proof water shoes
- Hat, sunglasses, sunscreen, towel

As you investigate the tide pools, look for the two different forms of barnacle: stalked and sessile. If you find the stalked type, study the tree-like form and imagine how the legend of the barnacle tree came to be.

Walking over the rocks, notice the natural skid-proofing shells: these are most likely a form of sessile barnacle. Stop to study their structure. Consider the barnacle's life cycle. Imagine this animal as a babe, in its cypris form, searching for this exact spot to grow old. Study its calcium carbonate shell. Feel the texture. With a hand lens, observe the center of the volcano-like cone, and find the door plates—the terga and scuta.

Find a tide pool filled with water, yet safe from wave break. Take time to observe the pool. It may appear empty, but your lack of movement will encourage theirs (the creatures in the pool will not move until the movement of shadows above subsides—predator avoidance behavior). Scan the cast of creatures and focus on a barnacle. Watch the barnacle for a few minutes. A feeding barnacle is evidenced by the waving feathery appendages, or cirri. Imagine the "leg net" encircling and netting its catch, as it pulls the invisible prey to its mouth. Relax in the rhythm of the routine. Thank God for this unique being that teaches us to slow down and cling.

Promise of Hope

"So do not fear; for I am with you; do not be dismayed, for I am your God. I will strengthen you and help you; I will uphold you with my righteous right hand" (Isaiah 41:10).

PART IV
Gifts of the Mountains

"Climb the mountains and get their good tidings. Nature's peace will flow into you as sunshine flows into trees. The winds will blow their own freshness into you, and the storms their energy, while cares will drop away from you like the leaves of Autumn."

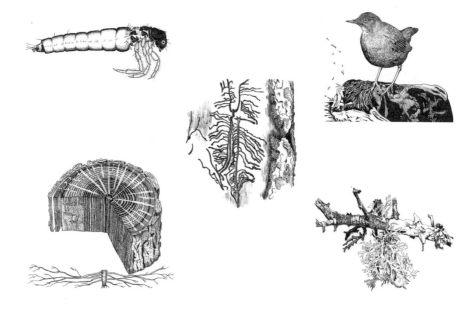

–John Muir

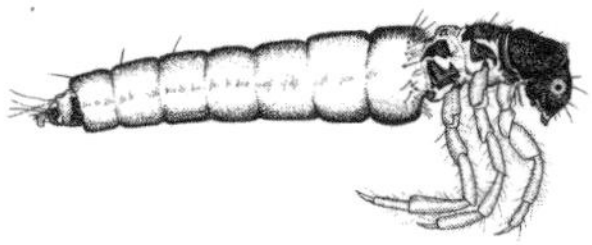

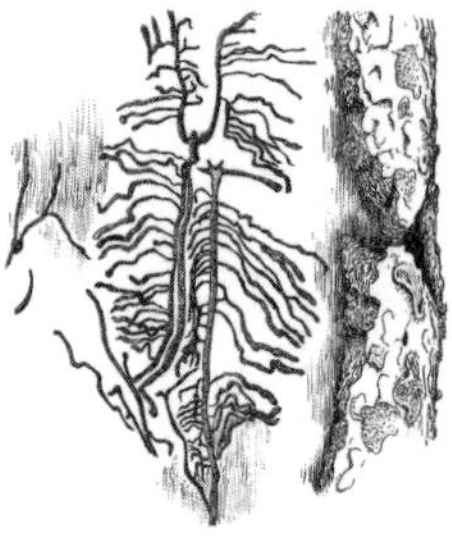

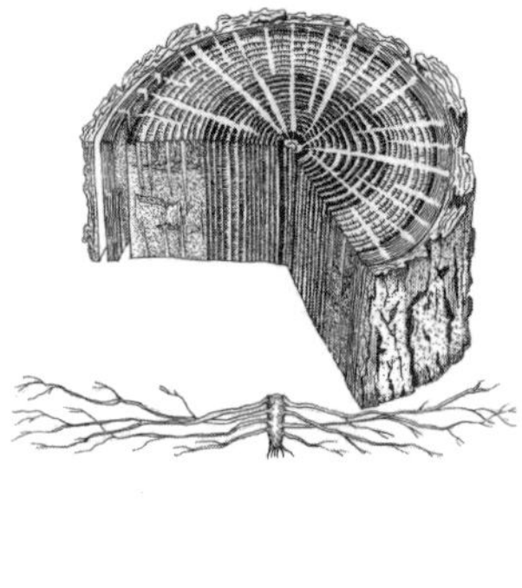

15
A UNIQUE TWEET
The American Dipper

"He must sing though the heavens fall." -John Muir

Here's a riddle for you to consider.

> I am a 'singularly joyous and loveable little fellow ... clad in a waterproof suit ... smoothly plump.'[1] Who am I?

While it may sound like Santa in a rain slicker, the mysterious creature is actually the American Dipper, or Water Ouzel, as described by John Muir, an American naturalist. A most unusual bird, the American Dipper (*Cinclus mexicanus*), is a swimming songster known for belting out melody supreme.

The Dipper maintains a flock of eccentricities—curious dipping movements, amphibious vision, and diving skills, to name a few—that rival a cliff diver. All this wonder comes wrapped up in a regular robin-sized bird that is equipped to survive and even thrive in harsh environments. The Dipper is one unique tweet.

Don't we all have a bit of Dipper in us—those eccentricities that make me, me and you, you? We should learn to celebrate our uniqueness.

After all, Muir was perhaps one of the greatest fans of North America's only aquatic songbird, and was a bit of an odd bird himself. Described as a "wild-haired, eccentric Scotsman fired with enthusiasm" for all things wild and wonderful, Muir burned with a passion for life that escapes most people.[2] Muir was devoted to the study of the American Dipper, known to him as the water ouzel, and collected ten years of observations. Muir dedicated an entire chapter to his feathered friend in his book *The Mountains of California*. I have to wonder if Muir's admiration for the Dipper was due to their similar lifestyles: both managed to peck out an existence on the road less traveled—with Muir exploring rugged unexplored territories and the Dipper exploiting a habitat no songbird in its right feather would dare to fly—or swim.

The submarine songbird dives into the chilled chaos of rivers and forages for insects. The Dipper appears surprisingly comfortable navigating the waters, swimming not with webbed feet, but strong "flipper-like" muscular wings. When the Dipper pops back up to the surface, water zips down its back due to its enlarged "oil preen" gland, a whopping ten percent larger than that of other songbirds. Other standard features on this land-bird-turned-swimmer include insulated feathers, closeable nostril tabs, and lens-like swim goggles. Clearly, the Dipper was born to dive.

I can't say the same of my underwater endeavors. As a child, I spent summers diving for lake treasures, which usually left me choking and sputtering with a nose full of water. That's not so for the Dipper who is endowed with a nifty nostril flap that conveniently closes upon diving. In addition, as I struggled to see the shine of the coins sans swim goggles, the Dipper sports its own built-in lens of sorts, a third lens which horizontally covers the eye much as a sliding glass door is closed. To top it off, the lens of the Dipper's eye has shape-shifting qualities typically possessed only by diving birds, enabling them to retain focus underwater.

Biologists Katzir and Howland noted that diving birds have a curved cornea which has the unique ability to flex. It literally bulges and oozes under the direction of highly developed eye muscles to compensate for the altered light-bending qualities under water.[3] And, oddly enough, the Dipper, which is technically a land bird, is equipped with a squishy cornea possessing a range of motion four times greater than that of the humble chicken. We humans might as well be chickens—for we too possess a flat, less flexible cornea, which suits us just fine for our life above water.

The dapper Dipper, however, requires these unusual characteristics to carve out a living in its unique habitat. Can you picture our creative, Inventor God in his workshop conjuring up this delightful little bird that would live along the river and dine in its depths? Can you hear him saying to the pre-incarnate Jesus (yep, he was there at creation; check out Proverbs 8:30 and 1 Corinthians 1:24, 30):

> 'Let's make him a songbird of the river, with wings protected by oil for swimming, and with goggle-like eyes to forage under the water.'

Okay, so I'm using my wild imagination. But, biblically, I am on

THE AMERICAN DIPPER
(Cinclus mexicanus)

solid ground. Just read the conversation God had with Job regarding the wonders of creation in Job 38 and 39. Then tell me God does not have an active sense of imagination. God is Creator; we acknowledge that. But our Creator God is also a brilliant inventor.

In a similar, yet much smaller vein, John Muir invented. Not living wonders, but great creative gadgets. The "early rising machine" is one of my personal favorites. This device—a glorified alarm clock bed—cleverly and conveniently dumped Muir out of bed at the appointed time.[4] Other ingenious inventions ranged from barometers to waterwheels and demonstrated that Muir loved to tinker.

Muir also toyed with the direction of his life and considered invention as a livelihood. But it was an accident in a carriage wheel shop that would cause him to pursue his passion and discover his destiny. Late one night while Muir tightened belts on a machine, a file slipped from his hands and was sent airborne. He literally felt the light drain from his eye as the file found and pierced his eye. Temporary blindness resulted.

In a Pauline fashion, this experience inspired further contemplation. As Muir spent a month confined to bed in a darkened room, the purpose of his life came to light. Author Dennis Williams said of Muir:

> He became convinced more than ever that life itself was the only true wealth and that the spiritual side of life was much more important in the end than the material.[5]

Muir decided to read the power and goodness of God written in nature while roaming through the wilds. Over the course of his lifetime, he explored the wilds. Little did he know his journals and his journeys would change the way we see the natural world. Sometimes we must lose our sight to gain vision. Vision provides perspective in life.

The Dipper's amphibious vision—the ability to see both above and below the water—is advantageous to a diving land bird. We would do well to take a lesson from the Dipper and develop amphibious vision of our own, and view life on earth through the lens of heaven. Though at times our earthly situation may appear dire, we must lift our eyes heavenward, off of the problem and on to the hope we have in Christ Jesus. Consider the words of Paul, a man who experienced the trauma of temporary blindness,

> I pray also that the eyes of your heart may be enlightened in order that

> you may know the hope to which he has called you, the riches of his glorious inheritance in the saints.[6]

Perhaps we are blinded by a fog of fear and doubt. Or clouds of concern and worry. We need to employ amphibious vision—where we lift our eyes above our problems and add a God dimension to our sight.

> I lift up my eyes to the hills—where does my help come from? My help comes from the LORD, the Maker of heaven and earth (Psalm 121: 1-2).

This "amphi-vision" will lift us from our fog of fear, in spite of our difficulties.

While the Dipper appears to dance with its curious dipping motion for which it is named, the exact reason for the jig remains unclear. Various theories abound on the cause of the dip—from camouflage (the backdrop of the moving stream allows the bird to blend in) to communication (a "dance of exuberance, born of joy of living along sparkling mountain streams").[7] Though poetic and romantic, the biologist in me says the dance bit is pushing it. I'm okay with the fact that the purpose of the dance remains unclear. I prefer to enjoy the song, which can elicit joy from even the most taciturn.

Muir's own spirits were buoyed by this little bird. On numerous occasions he credits the Dipper with cheering him in his solitary wanderings:

> I have often been delighted to see a pure, spiritual glow come into the countenances of hard business men and old miners, when a songbird chanced to alight near them.[8]...
>
> Nearly all of his music is sweet and tender...breaking farther on into a sparkling form of melodious notes, which glow with subdued enthusiasm.[9]

But perhaps more than the beauty of the song itself is the fact that the songbird sang despite the conditions surrounding him:

> However dark and boisterous the weather, snowing, blowing or cloudy, all the same he sings, and with never a note of sadness. No need of spring sunshine to thaw his song, for it never freezes.[10]

Nearly 130 years later, scientists are studying that very concept—the effect of song on mood. According to Eleanor Ratcliffe, researcher at the University of Surrey,

> A great deal of anecdotal evidence suggests that we respond positively to birdsong. However, currently there is a lack of scientific research on the psychological effects of listening to birds.[11]

Ratcliffe plans to conduct a three-year study to evaluate the impact of birdsongs on mood, attention and creativity. Perhaps the research will conclude what Muir seemed to know all along:

> Everybody needs beauty as well as bread, places to play in and pray in, where nature may heal and give strength to body and soul.

Nature is restorative. In studying God's creation, not only are we restored and refreshed, but we can learn a lesson in accepting our uniqueness. God in his infinite wisdom created each of us as unique beings. On purpose.

> You created my inmost being; you knit me together in my mother's womb. I praise you because I am fearfully and wonderfully made (Psalm 139:13).

So do we praise him for our eccentricities? Do we thank him for our seemingly imperfect ways, such as the Dipper who, though he is born with "dry-bird" feet, is an exquisite swimmer? What self-perceived flaw do you fret about? In my own life, I struggled for years to develop "schmoozability." I longed for the ability to be gregarious and outgoing. Yet all the while I remain a deeply solitary, introverted soul. Coming to terms with my introspective nature allowed me to be me. My introspective qualities fuel my ability to research and write. And for that, I am grateful.

Accepting who we are and how we were created is half the battle. God doesn't make mistakes. We are fearfully, wonderfully, and uniquely made. Why? "For we are God's workmanship, created in Christ Jesus to do good works, which God prepared in advance for us to do" (Ephesians 2:10). The lesson comes not in longing for who we think we should have been created to be, but in living who we *are* created to be.

Your life bears the signature of the master. What more could you want?

WONDERCISE

Dipper Watch

Time spent on a river can be cathartic. Plant yourself on its banks and allow the tumbling waters to unwind the tension in your life. If, by chance, you are entertained by the Dipper, you are doubly blessed. While worldwide there are five species of Dippers, North America is home to one species, and this is confined to western regions.

If you are bird watching in the West, listen for the sweet song of the American Dipper.

Knapsack Needs:

- Field guide to birds for your area
- Binoculars
- Camera (optional)

Watch the grey, stocky bird for the following behaviors:

The characteristic dip—a bobbing up and down motion in which they quickly lower their entire body, almost like a dance move. How many dips do you count per minute? Dipping rates are believed to increase when Dippers are agitated.

The swim
The dive
The song—melodic and elaborate

Notice its constant motion—dipping, darting, crouching, wading, running, swimming, snorkeling, preening

Contemplate the characteristics of this unique bird. Thank God for your own unique characteristics. Praise him for the wonder of his ways.

Promise of Hope

"I praise you because I am fearfully and wonderfully made; your works are wonderful, I know that full well" (Psalm 139:14).

16

COMFORT ZONES & CADDISFLY HOMES

"Living at risk is jumping off the cliff and building your wings on the way down."
-Ray Bradbury

In the caddisfly world, living at risk is releasing your naked caterpillar-like body into the river's wild and capricious currents and sprouting wings on the way up. And you thought human adolescence was brutal! Let me explain.

First off, if the term *caddisfly* brings to mind the image of the lowly and despised house fly, think again. The caddis is no ordinary fly. With its silky wings propped up over its body like a miniature pup tent, this moth-esque insect is more closely related to moths and butterflies than true flies. Roughly twelve thousand species of the delicate, winged wonders have been described. The fact that their moth-like wings are covered with hairs, not scales, is reflected in their scientific name of *Trichoptera*, derived from the Greek *trichos* meaning "hair," and *ptera* meaning "wings." While the terrestrial adult form of the insect sports silk-haired wings and flies about, it is the magical, mystical aquatic larval form that fascinates me most.

Worldwide there are roughly fifteen thousand species of caddisflies. And while the caddisfly occupies just a tiny niche in this wide, wide world, it is a key cog in the wheel of life. The caddisfly is an important food source for fish and other aquatic predators. In addition, the caddisfly serves a key role in processing organic materials in the aquatic ecosystem.

Let's venture into this two-dimensional world of the caddisfly.

The life cycle of the caddisfly begins with the ephemeral female laying her eggs in water. The eggs hatch into aquatic larvae. Each larva then builds its own shelter using self-spun, waterproof silk adhesive. While some caddis are indeed without a case (think slug), most do carry a case

CADDISFLY

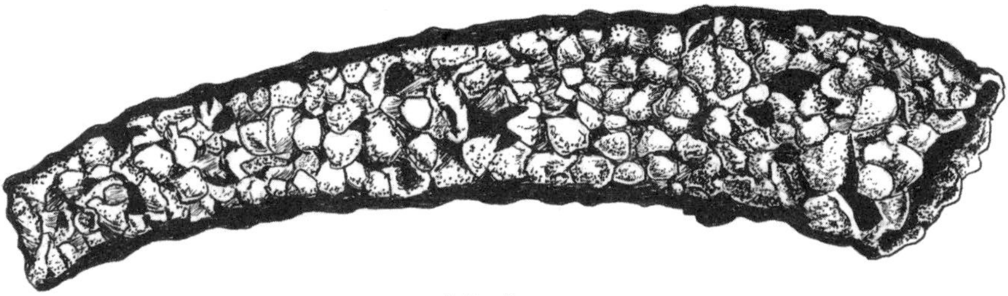

Caddisfly case

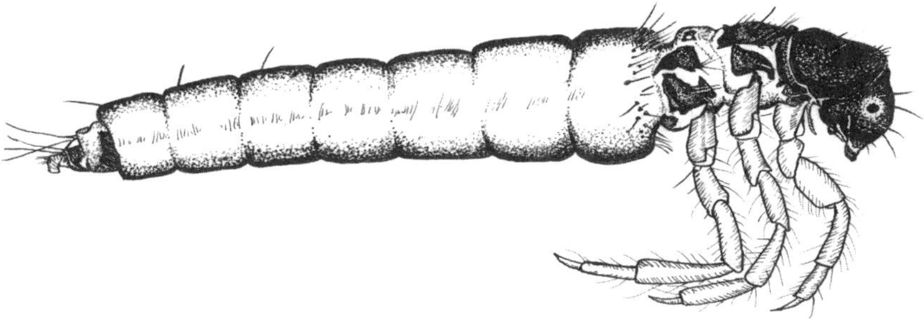

Caddisfly larva

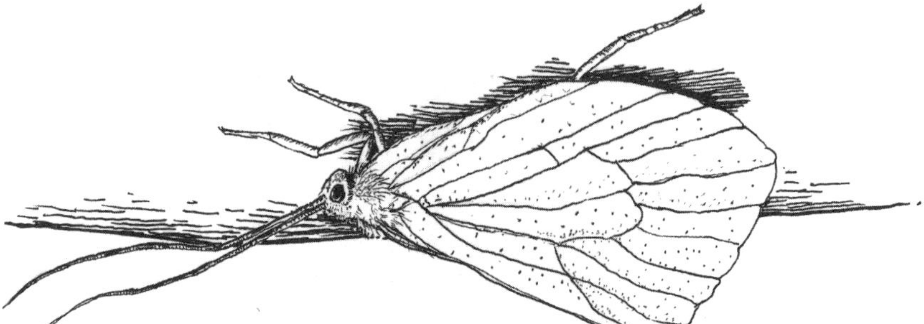

Caddisfly adult

(think snail). The case designs are diverse and each species constructs one from specific materials. I guess you can judge a caddisfly by its cover.

The common name *caddisfly* is believed to come from *cadezs*, a term that harkens to the Shakespearean era and refers to a ribbon of yarn sold by street vendors. To advertise their wares, these "caddice men" often stitched samples of their textile trims to their overcoats. In the same way, the caddisfly spins a silk coat or case, and embellishes it with bits of sticks and stones, debris or leaves.

Imagine, beneath the waters of streams, rivers, lakes and ponds lives a silk-spinning, sand-castle-building master of sorts. Using a gland (spinnerette) near its mouth, these unique insects spin a silk tape of sorts to construct their "castle" and affix its building material of choice. Various aquatic items are recycled in caddisfly home construction—pebbles, sand grains, sticks or leaves. Using scraps of this and that, caddisfly larvae construct elaborate homes. There's no case like home.

Caddisflies are creative or resourceful, depending on how you see it. If you take away their building material of choice and provide a substitute, they will build. This was confirmed by Ben Stoudt, director of environmental studies at Wheeling Jesuit University and twenty-year student of caddisflies. Stoudt wondered what would happen if you substituted the given materials of dirt and debris with something like pearls, diamonds, and rubies. Would you get a jeweled case? Stoudt decided to find out. Two and a half years and six experiments later, Stoudt's stone artist produced the precursor to gemstone homes: a case of colored aquarium gravel. Inspired by the results, Stoudt increased the wager and added turquoise. Success. Currently, the works of art are available in materials ranging from abalone shell to gold nuggets, from emeralds to rubies.

If given the goods, caddisflies build jeweled homes. But no matter the material, the caddisfly spends childhood at home as a caddis larva, in the comfort zone of the stone (or twig) castle. Looking like a mermaid of sorts, the top half of its body protrudes from the case and the vulnerable lower half is enclosed in the elongated tube. The caddisfly larva passes time for months in this stage. Living comfortably. When threatened, it simply withdraws into its cave of sticks where it stays till the danger passes.

Childhood can't last forever, not even in a bug's life. The time to transition to adulthood eventually arrives. Unless the larva releases itself into the current, it will remain forever a babe, forever stunted in immaturity. Forever trapped in the cave. The journey is not without risk, yet the rewards are great. So the larva withdraws into its case and seals the opening in preparation for the next stage: a wild and risky rollercoaster ride to the surface and the wings of adulthood. Gary LaFontaine, author of *Caddisflies*, describes it this way:

> Once out of the silk-lined, stone or vegetable cocoon, drifting freely in the stream, the swimming caddisfly emergent begins inflating its surrounding skin with gas bubbles and beating with hair-fringed legs, both of these actions lifting the insect up through the water. At the surface, the adult hesitates, pushing against the underside of the meniscus (surface film) and struggling to shed the pupal skin. … Once free, it takes off after a preliminary hop or two.[1]

The liquid ascent to freedom is no easy swim. Drifting at the mercy of the current, the insect must also dodge the gauntlet of predacious trout who drool at the thought of caddisfly hatch. And, according to LaFontaine, the energy required to pierce the surface waters is equivalent to "the amount of energy needed for a full-grown person to escape if he were covered with three feet of dirt." The whole scenario is drenched in risk.

Often times, our own lives require that we embrace risk during life's transitions: a move, a job change, or a health issue. Transition periods are fraught with decisions that require difficult choices. I love that the Bible is full of examples of those who faced difficult choices, took a risk—and triumphed. Consider the story of Joshua, the leader of Operation Transition.

Years ago, God promised the Israelites land. Lots of it. And not just any old hunk of dirt. This land was a land of Promise. A land of freedom. Yet somehow, overcome with cares and a healthy dose of stubborn disobedience, they allowed the promise to wither. The dream disappeared. God, however, renewed his promise in the person of Joshua.

Even with Joshua as their leader, the Israelites faced a problem. A river of a problem. The Israelites lived life wandering on the "safe" side of the river—no giants, no armies, and no risk. The promised land lay just beyond the river on the other side. The Israelites had to make a choice. Would they cross the river and risk death in order to claim the promise?

Joshua's life up to this point reveals a resume of God-appointed incidents, designed to prepare him for this stage in the journey:

- Survived slavery in Egypt
- Witnessed God's power through plagues
- Participated in the Great Escape through the Red Sea
- Climbed the holy mountain with Moses
- One of two smart spies (out of ten) that scoped out the promised land

Now God brought Joshua and the nation to the brink of a river bank at flood stage. The risk level is off the charts. Once Moses's right-hand man, now the burden of responsibility lay square on Joshua's shoulders. Joshua faced the gargantuan task of leading the clan into the Promised Land. Was he ready to accept the very real risk that would yield a fantastic future?

I can't help but smile when I read God's words to Joshua: "Moses my servant is dead." So much for introductory icebreakers. I think I would have started with a gentler, "Joshua, are you sitting down?" But God, being God, cuts to the chase:

> Now then, you and all these people get ready to cross the Jordan River into the land I am about to give them (Joshua 1:2).

I wonder if Joshua's mind screamed, *What? Cross the river? Now, at this time of year? Are you crazy? The river is at flood stage!* Though his mind might have screamed, I picture his face serene with a smile and a nod. Though Joshua may have choked on the assignment, he swallowed the assurance of God's promise of protection:

> As I was with Moses, so I will be with you; I will never leave you nor forsake you. … Be strong and courageous. … Be strong and *very* (emphasis mine) courageous (Joshua 1:5-7).

No doubt, God implied it would be difficult. And dangerous.

As if God is reading Joshua's mind (remember the Lord can read minds), he adds a final bit of advice:

> Do not be terrified, do not be discouraged for the Lord your God will be with you wherever you go (Joshua 1:9).

Wow! Such a promise. Such companionship for the challenge ahead.

Despite the risk, Joshua chose to obey God and leave the comfort zone. He accepted the risk. He knew it didn't involve smooth sailing on a slow river, but a jump in the white water at flood stage. Reaching for God's hand, Joshua jumped. He let go of fear and he let God lead. Geronimo, Joshua.

We should do the same. Sometimes, we just need to let go and leave. Leave doubt. Leave fear. Leave insecurity. Grab hold of God. And let him lead.

God leads by issuing specific instructions:

> When you see the ark of the covenant of the LORD your God … you are to move out from your positions and follow it. Then you will know which way to go since you have never been this way before (Joshua 3:3-4).

Joshua did not know the way. We must remember that God promises to go before us. He directs our path. He is the lead man. We don't need to know the way, only believe that he does. We only need to follow. God knows the way. Even though it looks rough. Even though it looks uncertain. Even though it doesn't make sense to step into a river at flood stage.

Notice God's direct order. "When you reach the edge of the Jordan's waters, go and stand in the river" (Joshua 3:8). Stand in it. Not admire from the bank. Not wait till waters recede. But GO and STAND in the river. And therein lies the rub. Or the risk. And the test. God is asking the Israelites to trust his wisdom and follow his directions, though the way is unclear.

The command seems crazy. Step into the deluge of out-of-control water. And linger there. Again, my version of this story would have me asking God, "Why not just stop the waters before I step in? Please? Pretty please?" Yet, the test of our faith comes in the act of stepping into the storm armed with the knowledge that he goes before us, even when the waters are too choppy to see. Blind faith. And wouldn't you know it, as soon as

> their feet touched the water's edge, the water from upstream stopped flowing. It piled up in a heap a great distance away … so the people crossed over (Joshua 3:15-17).

If the Israelites hadn't followed God's lead and God's directions, they would have been trapped on the wrong side of the river in the "un-promised" land. We must trust. And obey. For there is no other way.

STONES OF REMEMBRANCE

I wear a stone necklace fashioned by God's insect artist, the caddisfly.[2] The stone case that adorns my neck reminds me that God promises to go before me in all the scary stuff of life. I stole the idea from Joshua.

Post traumatic river crossing, Joshua used stones to serve as a reminder of the day God provided the Israelites' safe passage. The stones served as a "sign among you"—a sign to remember and share with future generations that God keeps his promises. And we would do well to remember all that God has done and promises to do. Read Hebrews chapter 11 and refresh your memory of the heroes of faith and what they accomplished with God at the helm of their lives.

God has flight in mind for the young caddisfly's future, but unless the larva lets go, it remains trapped. We often don't realize we are confined in our fears until we relax into the currents of life and let God carry us across the raging river. This is tough to do. As humans, we like roadmaps and insurance plans. And money back guarantees. Yet in life, the only guarantee we have is the God guarantee. He promises to go with us. In the currents of uncertainty, in the wild river of life's journey, he promises to carry us. We only need to let go of that which tethers, so we may fly!

WONDERCISE

Enter the Water

As Joshua and his group camped on the banks of the Jordan River, imagine their surroundings: cattails, willows, and cottonwoods; warblers, woodpeckers, and waterfowl; dragonflies, gnats, and yes, even mosquitoes. Upriver the beaver built its dam, a frog bellowed on the banks. This community of creatures and its non-living components (rocks, soils, and the river itself) are connected to form an ecosystem.

Knapsack Needs:

- Hand lens
- Footwear that can get wet
- Long-sleeved shirt to protect from possible mosquitoes
- Sunglasses and/or sunhat

Sit on the bank of a river and contemplate the river life and ecosystem. Then step into the stream (yes, you'll get wet). Search for caddisflies. Look under the water for larvae and pupae. Gently lift a rock or piece of wood from the water and with your hand lens examine for larvae and pupae. The cases constructed of nondescript sand grains or a mixed bag of plant material are difficult to describe in detail. Generally, you are looking for a small tube-shaped case, the size of a half-inch strand of pasta noodle. Color will vary. Return the rock to the same position and location under the water, taking care not to disrupt the habitat or vegetation.

Depending on your luck, you may have found a caddisfly case. Or perhaps you saw a fish, frog, or fly. Realize that this community of creatures and the ground and water in which they live are connected, each individual part of the whole. And God has the whole world in his hands. He cares for us. All of us.

Promise of Hope

"When you pass through the waters, I will be with you; and when you pass through the rivers, they will not sweep over you" (Isaiah 43:2).

17
SUPERHERO LICHENS

"Coming together is a beginning. Keeping together is progress. Working together is success." -Henry Ford

Superman: if he were a plant, he would be a lichen. Caped wonders of the natural world, lichens can split a rock, survive freezing temperatures, and feed the world—of sparrows and squirrels. Lichens are wonders.

But unlike Superman, lichens do not work alone; instead they function more as a superhero combo, a Batman and Robin dynamic duo of sorts. While many consider lichens to be plants, technically lichens are classified in the kingdom, Fungi.

Two individuals, a fungus and algae, are woven together as one in a symbiotic (mutually beneficial) relationship. The fungal component serves as shelter for the algae providing protection from the elements, desiccation, and certain predators. The algae, in return, provide food for the fungus through its ability to convert sunlight, carbon dioxide and water into usable energy. This give and take relationship reminds me of holy matrimony (minus the fungus and algae, of course).

I'm not alone. Patricia Lichen, naturalist and author, considered the unique blend of algae and fungus while contemplating her own upcoming union.

> Rather than using only one of our last names, or combining them (which would have resulted in the unwieldy 'Delano-Hutchinson'), we decided to choose a new family name.[1]

Lichen fit the bill. She and her husband often told a story about Freddy Fungus and Alice Algae to explain the lichen relationship.

> Freddy Fungus provides the structure for a home, and Alice Algae would produce food. It seems they took a likin' to each other.[2]

LICHEN

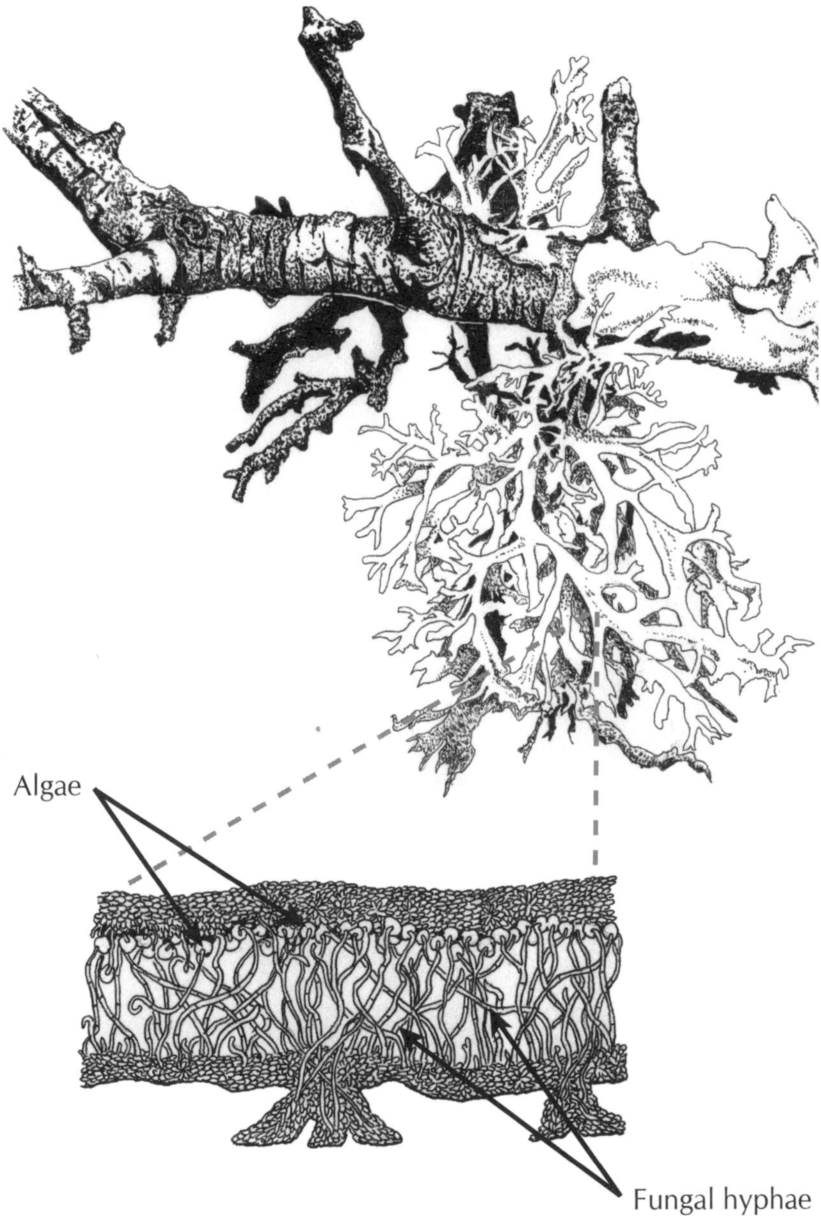

Lichen And Its Microscopic Structure

The team of naturalists decided this story symbolized their own relationship, hence they chose the surname, Lichen, to define themselves. Cute.

I wish I could say my husband and I were that creative. When we married in 1981, we too wanted our surname to symbolize unity. We filled out the necessary paperwork, paid a nominal fee and appeared in court before a judge to officially combine our existing names—O'Connor and Casey—to become O'Casey. While I can't say the name is as descriptive as Lichen, it certainly symbolizes two unique individuals joined together as one, complete with their very profound differences. And how.

Sometimes I imagine God as cosmic comedian, joining men and women in holy matrimony. I mean, what was he thinking? Men, with their testosterone-driven, conquest oriented and very compartmentalized lives paired with women and their estrogen-driven, nurture-centered and multitask-geared lives coming together as one. Really? It must be God's plan, because no human in their right mind would deem it plausible. However, like the fungal and algal lichen team, the unlikely union of the male and female human species in marriage can yield a sweet dynamic duo—albeit not without lots of prayer and understanding.

While the husband and wife relationship requires sacrificial serving in a multitude of ways, lichens participate in sharing the basics: food and shelter. As lichenologist Trevor Goward explains, "Lichens are fungi that have discovered agriculture."[3] Today, this symbiotic relationship is well documented and accepted. However, the road to this discovery was paved with rejection and redirection, as Beatrix Potter discovered. That's right. *That* Beatrix Potter, creator of the famed *Peter Rabbit.*

What most bunny-loving readers don't know is that before Potter became a noted children's author and artist, she lived the curious, industrious, and intelligent life of a self-taught mycologist—a fancy name for fungus researcher. Fascinated by the structure and function of lichens, Potter set up a lab in her kitchen. There she began culturing, observing, dissecting and drawing algal and fungal spores. She documented her findings in hundreds of detailed watercolors—hand drawn at six hundred times magnification.

Potter's extensive research convinced her of the symbiotic relationship between fungi and algae. She was the first person in Britain to discover this connection. An ocean channel away, a Swiss botanist, Simon Schwendener, was also a proponent of the symbiotic theory. But the two lone rangers—amateur scientist and professional botanist—professed an unpopular theory.

Determined to change some minds, Beatrix Potter had a plan. Potter, an earth-is-round kinda gal in the flat-topped, male-dominated scientific world of her day, submitted a paper, "On the Germination of the Spores of Agaricinaeae" on April 1, 1897 to the Linnean Society of London. Because women were not allowed to attend these meetings, Potter's paper was read in her absence. The members in attendance were not convinced by her findings. Snubbed by the scientific community, Potter's theory was shown the door. As the door slammed shut, it trapped the tail of her idea on the way out, holding it hostage for years.

Linda Lear recounts the event in *Beatrix Potter: A Life in Nature*:

> The Linnean Society did not reject Potter's paper because they never seriously considered it. … Beatrix Potter was too insignificant a player for the botanical establishment to be concerned with. … The establishment scientists simply discounted her research and ignored her conclusions.[4]

The words "too insignificant a player" echo in my mind. Would that story have ended differently had Potter been part of a team of scientists with a common goal? Perhaps. And while we don't know Potter's thoughts or state of mind post-rejection, we do know she redirected her efforts. Just a few short years later, in 1901, her first book, *The Tale of Peter Rabbit* was published and became an overnight success.

Potter's life story demonstrates her tenacity. I find it ironic that the very subject she dedicated years of research to—Lichens—are themselves a study in tenacity. Let's explore lichens—their wonder and their ability to endure.

Like a living tapestry of texture and color, lichens exhibit endless diversity. Based on their body type, lichens can be divided into three predominant forms:

1. ***Foliose***: Think foliage. This type of lichen is two dimensional, flattened and leaf-like in structure.

2. ***Fruticose*** (shrubby lichens): With shrub-like growth, fruticose lichens grow in three dimensions and appear as little bushes sprouting from the surface of rocks and trees.

3. *Crustose* (crusties): This form of lichen appears to be painted on its substrate forming crust-like blotches. In bonding tightly to the surface, crustose lichens are difficult to remove from their substrate—much like a quart of paint that has spilled and hardened on the sidewalk.

Lichen forms are unique and their impact on the ecosystem is great. Check out these amazing attributes:

- **Globetrotters**: It seems no land is off limits to lichens. Lichens can be found on every continent on the planet. They survive in the frigid climate of the arctic as well as in the sun-baked tropics.

- **Soil Restorers**: Over time, lichens—nature's grunt workers—can restore life to nutrient-drained soils. When their root-like threads, called rhizines, combine with silt, dust, and water, lichens mechanically exert pressure and slowly penetrate tiny rock crevices, working to crack the mighty boulder. In addition, lichens may act on rocks chemically. Some lichens exude a small amount of acid which reacts with its mineral substrate, causing a gradual dissolution of rock and transforming it into soil.

- **Wildlife Sustainers**: Rich in carbohydrates, lichens provide a food source for animals that feed on them. Deer, squirrels, and chipmunks depend on the lichen for food. Scientists have documented some fifty species of birds that rely on lichens as their favored nesting material.

- **Pollution Monitors**: While tolerant of heat and cold extremes, lichens are very sensitive to pollutants. As such, lichens thrive in the clean air of wide open spaces of forests, mountains and deserts, but are sparse in urban areas. Valued as bio-indicators, lichens can serve as useful tools to determine air quality, much like a canary does for a coal mine.

Lichens possess an impressive list of features. But what impresses me most is their unique structure. The body of a lichen is composed of a fungus and an algae (green or blue-green). On its own, a fungus is unable to produce food and must rely on other organisms for nutrients. Yet in lichen form, woven within its frame are strands of algae which thrive on the arms of the fungus and operate a sort of fast-food joint, doling out the carbs via photosynthesis.

Such an unusual arrangement allows the lichen to expand its territory into a great diversity of habitats that neither fungus nor algae could conquer as individuals. Sort of a "united we stand, divided we fall" approach. Lichens are nature's poster child for symbiosis.

Imagine what we could accomplish as a church if we approached ministry with the symbiotic style of the lichen. Such a lichen way of life is biblical:

> As it is, there are many parts, but one body. The eye cannot say to the hand, 'I don't need you!' And the head cannot say to the feet, 'I don't have need of you!' On the contrary, those parts that seem to be weaker are indispensable … so that there should be no division in the body but that its parts should have equal concern for each other (1 Corinthians 12:20-25).

The church that values the unique contributions of each member will expand their territory and better serve the needs of others.

That's teamwork on a community level. Let's consider teamwork on a personal level. Just as team lichen thrives in harsh conditions, we can thrive in the difficulties of life if we team up with the Master himself. He invites us to join him.

> Come to me, all you who are weary and burdened, and I will give you rest. Take my yoke upon you and learn from me, for I am gentle and humble in heart, and you will find rest for your souls. For my yoke is easy and my burden is light (Matthew 11:28-30).

What is he asking us to do? Partner with him. In the agrarian society of Jesus' day, the term "yoke" referred to a device built for two oxen. Yoked together, the oxen functioned as a unit, with the older, more experienced ox bearing the heaviest part of the burden and teaching the younger ox the way. Jesus invites us to hop into his harness as we navigate the rocky roads of life together, with him bearing more of the burden.

That is the lifestyle I long for. Of course, it means I must get over myself. Lose the pride. Relinquish my rugged individualism. Daily I must remember to partner with the Master and depend on him to see me through. David reminds us of this in Psalm 18:29:

> With your help, I can advance against a troop; with my God I can scale a wall.

With God by our side, there is nothing we cannot do. His power enables us to endure life's sometimes inhospitable conditions and live the tenacious life.

It's teamwork of the supernatural kind. And it beats the partnership of Batman and Robin or fungus and algae.

Jesus and me. Jesus and you. Now that's a team worth joining.

WONDERCISE

Lichen Hunt

Lichens are rarely city dwellers. Look for lichens on a trip to the mountains, the desert, or on the undeveloped coast. If you are fortunate to live in a rural area, you may find lichens in your own backyard.

Knapsack Needs:

- Hand Lens
- Local field guide to Lichens (optional)

A brief survey of my property revealed a rich lichen tapestry woven into the landscape in a vast variety of color, sizes and shapes. Lichens are unobtrusive and often go unnoticed. Once you discover a few, your eyes key in to them and will begin to see them in many places: on rocks, bark, dead branches, a wall, or a fence. Old tombstones are known to yield colorful crops of lichens. Start looking and you will be amazed by their variety. With a hand lens you will gain a greater appreciation for the lowly lichen.

As you explore, consider the following questions:

1. How would you describe its color?
2. On what type of substrate is it growing? Rock? Live tree bark? Dead twig?

Lichens have been described as goblets, pixie cups, ruffled, scalloped, horn-like, witch hair, beard-like. Use your imagination to describe the lichens you see. Enter your observations in your notebook.

Promise of Hope

"And in him you too are being built together to become a dwelling in which God lives by his Spirit" (Ephesians 2:22).

Let's resolve to live lichen-like, joined together with and dependent upon God to provide all we need. Together the possibilities are endless.

18
Beetles, Tattoos & Love

Asked by a theologian what could be inferred about the mind of the Creator from a study of His works, the British scientist J.B.S. Haldane dryly replied, "an inordinate fondness for beetles."[1]

Fondness for beetles? That's so God. Most of us don't feel the love. Some do, however, profess a certain attraction to beetles. Consider the bizarre beetle caper of 2010. Seems a woman entering Brownsville, Texas from Mexico stirred up a beetle's nest at the border. Her car (for the sake of a good story, imagine her driving a Volkswagen Beetle) crawled past the stares of inquiring agents. All at once her jewelry jumped. Border patrol agents zoomed in for a closer look. Her broach was bugged. Literally. In the end, border patrol agents confiscated her live bejeweled beetle broach. No joke. The beetle sported an assortment of gemstones and was tethered to her sweater with a gold chain. The crime? The woman failed to obtain the proper "pest-y" paperwork. Nonetheless, she was released unharmed. I can't say the same for the beetle. To say that beetles can attract attention is an understatement.

Beetles represent one-fourth of all living animals and inhabit the inhospitable. From polar ice caps to the Sahara Desert, the beetle is the king. Scientists estimate that more than 350,000 species of beetles have been identified with more being described each day.

Beetle diversity—in form and function—provides plenty of fodder for a round of beetle trivia. Check out these trivia (not trivial) tidbits:

- The title for the heaviest beetle goes to the goliath beetle who weighs in just shy of a quarter pound and stretches to nearly a half foot in length.
- An average-sized man can pull about 0.86 times his own weight, but a leaf beetle (*Donacia*) can pull 42.7 times its own weight."

GALLERY ENGRAVINGS

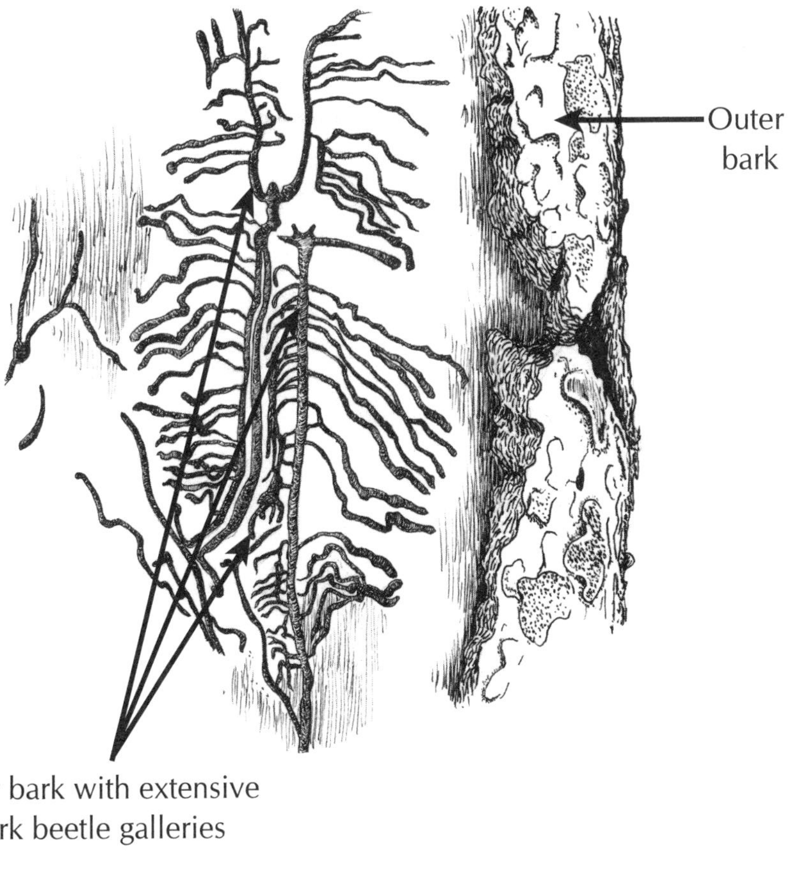

- Blister beetles have been used both as an aphrodisiac and to produce hair on bald heads.[2]

Sometimes trivia gets personal: I own (and even wear) beetle body part jewelry. Beetle wings make great earrings!

I realize that some of you may consider it natural for a biologist to find beetles fascinating. And I understand that most people who do not dig in the mud for a living are inclined to find beetles, shall we say, a bit intimidating. But if beetles push your panic button, hear this: Beetles cannot be ignored. I mean, how could they? Beetles crawl the earth. As a biologist, my bug-uciary duty demands I not sugarcoat beetles (although I've heard that in some cultures, chocolate-covered beetles are all the rage). I won't attempt to present beetles as sweet and adorable creatures you'll want to cuddle up with on the couch. They're not and you won't.

But for heaven's sake, beetles aren't out to get us. Beetles are a part of life. And biology, by its very definition means the study of life (*bio* = "life," *ology* = "the study of"). So how 'bout, just for this chapter, you agree to humor me and put aside any preconceived prejudices of the lowly beetle. Great. I thank you in advance for your cooperation. Prepare to enlarge your view of one of God's misunderstood creations.

Meet the pine engraver bark beetle (*Ips pini*), which looks remarkably like an espresso jelly bean with wings (okay, so I'm nearsighted). This species belongs to the clan of engraver beetles known for carving their signature on trees. Engraver bark beetles are named for their habit of gnawing their way through the protective cover of a tree—its outer bark—and carving wooden "cradles" in the inner bark, where their young develop. Let's bore into the life of a bark beetle.

The pine engraver is one of the most common bark beetles, setting up shop in thirteen of the western states. The adult male beetle moves into the tree and carves a "nuptial chamber." (Aren't some biology terms delightful?) He then spritzes the air with his personal brand of cologne (sort of a "Brut" for beetles), and entices a female to join him. The female honors her nesting instinct, enters the chamber, etches egg "cradles" into the bark and lays the eggs. The "cradles"—or in scientific jargon, galleries (how artsy)—are elaborate tunnels carved into the tree's living layer: the cambium.

Galleries come in a variety of shapes and styles. The western pine beetle toothes a free-spirited trail resembling cooked spaghetti. The mountain pine beetle, on the other hand, takes a more linear route, etching a vertical line with perpendicular cross tunnels. The fir engraver beetle etches a horseshoe-shaped gallery. Bottom line? You can judge—or at least attempt to classify—a beetle by its carving. Each engraving is specific to a particular species.

While these beetles etch their personal autograph on the trunk of the tree, the arboreal artist is not as innocent as it appears. Recently engraver bark beetles have taken heat for destroying entire forests. Before you pull the trigger on that can of bug spray to subdue the beast and save a tree, know this: bark beetles are crucial to the ecosystem for their role in decomposing dead and dying woody material.

Bark beetles are nature's recyclers and occur naturally within a forest ecosystem. To remove the beetle from the ecosystem is to stop the merry-go-round, or at least throw a wrench in the works. Considered "secondary pests," bark beetles "usually infest only stressed, weakened, damaged or downed pines."[3] Most researchers agree that the key to preventing bark beetle damage is to promote and maintain healthy forests. Occasionally the population of bark beetles will expand and overcome healthy trees, but this is not the norm.

Over the past century well-intentioned humans have entered the forests in grand numbers. In so doing, we have stepped onto the merry-go-round and changed its speed, altering forest structure and diversity. When we change a forest's natural diversity, toss in a dash of human produced pollution, and add a hint of climate change, the cumulative effect is trees with weakened resistance.

And the beetles are on high alert. They can smell stressed trees a mile away. Really, they can. According to Douglas Allen, professor of forest entomology, "Bark beetles could put a blood hound to shame!"[4] It seems these tiny beetles have a highly advanced sensory system which enables them to detect chemical odors emitted by a stressed tree.

And so they come. Like a thief looking for an easy target, beetles latch on, chew through the outer bark, and gain access to the tree's soft inner bark. The purpose of bark to a tree is protection. It is equivalent to our skin, and its job is to fend off attackers—germs that seek to invade and take us down.

In a perfect world, healthy trees fight back and throw a punch—of pitch, that sticky resinous liquid that trees produce when injured. The beetle either drowns in the toxic resins en route to the buried treasure, or abandons its efforts altogether. Trouble is, trees saddled with the effects of drought, pollution, or overcrowding have a crack in their armor. Their "pitching machine" is out of whack. This results in stands of trees branded with engravings that reflect the identity of the artist—its personal identification stamp—saying, "This is my work, my brood, my home." A savvy entomologist can identify the carver by the gallery. A particular style of engraving is characteristic of a particular species of beetle.

Somewhat similar is the art of engraving images onto the skin—tattoos—which reflect the beliefs and values of the adorned. The 2006 results of a Pew Research Poll revealed that one third of Americans between the ages of eighteen and forty sport a tattoo. And Christians are part of the trend. Young believers have hopped up on the table, bearing biceps, backs, and other body parts to share their faith with a cross, scripture or picture of Jesus emblazoned into their fleshly flesh.

This is nothing new. Coptic Christians have been known for centuries to declare their obedience and love for God through the tattoo. They longed to proclaim their allegiance to God, especially poignant during their times of intense persecution. Consider the view of Otto Meinardus, a Coptic scholar:

> There is no doubt that the principal purpose of the application of tattoos by the Copts serves their religious and ethnic identification … In times of persecution, the tattoo of the cross has given strength to the faithful and has made it impossible to deny their faith.[5]

And if you think that God above sits wagging a bony, shaming finger, consider this. God himself sports a tattoo. Uh-huh. I can prove it: "See, I have engraved you on the palms of my hands; your walls are ever before me" (Isaiah 49:16).

Engrave in Hebrew (*haqaq*) literally means to cut in or engrave in stone, as "hewing a tomb in the rock" and can be interpreted as "tattoo." God has tattooed each of us on his arm. In permanent, indelible ink. He will remember us. Forever.

But God doesn't need the tattoo to remind him of us. God thinks of us constantly. And loves us anyway. So much so that each one of us is uniquely engraved on the palm of the Father. No two tattoos are alike. Can you imagine our God with each of our names etched on his hand? God has some mighty big hands to hold all those names.

The holy and compassionate God has carved my name there. And yours. Why? To remind us that he will never forget us. His love is so grand that he goes to great lengths to declare it. And it must have been painful.

But that pain is but a mere twitch compared to the agony of watching his son die a brutal death, a nailed-to-the-cross death. Jesus suffered and died. But he rose again. And he came back and showed us his hands.

Remember when Jesus first appeared to his disciples? It was all about his hands. The doors were locked, yet he entered the room. In John chapter 20 Jesus gives Thomas a three point, hands-on lesson:

One: "Put your finger here; see my hands."

Two: "Reach out your hand and put it into my side."

Three: "Stop doubting, and believe."

Wise advice for us all. Jesus loves me, this I know. For the Bible tells me so. So do his nail pierced hands.

WONDERCISE

BARK BEAUTY

Trees are often distinguished by their bark. Two of my favorites are the mature ponderosa pine with its puzzle-piece bark and the white birch tree, which bears its bark in paper thin strips. In the shuffle of seasons a tree's bark can be overshadowed by spring's bloom, summer's fruit, or fall's foliage. When winter's starkness catapults bark into the spotlight, bundle up, step outside, and notice the rich tapestry of bark types God has created.

Knapsack Needs:

- Hand lens
- Field guide to local trees
- Field guide to local insects

Take a walk in your neighborhood and observe the following characteristics of tree bark:

- **Color**: Notice the variety in bark colors. List the different colors in your notebook and describe their rich hues.

- **Scent**: Some barks are richly aromatic. Take the time to smell the trees. Is the tree bark scented? If so, how would you describe the scent? Earthy? Sweet? Pungent?

- **Texture**: Observe the difference in bark forms: Are they thin and smooth, or rough and deeply furrowed? Using your hand lens, take a closer look at the intricate texture of the bark. Now get tactile and feel the difference between bark types. Describe this sensation in your notebook. Contemplate the wonder of bark, this layer of protection for the tree and a source of beauty in the gray of winter.

EXTRA-ORDINARY WONDER

On your next trip to the mountains, search for evidence of bark beetle engravings. Older forests usually have a number of dead and downed trees.

Peel loose some bark from several of these trees. With any luck, you may see the etching of a bark beetle—its characteristic signature. Using a local field guide to insects, and some detective work, try to match the carving to the beetle type.

Promise of Hope

"I will not forget you. See, I have engraved you on the palms of my hands; your walls are ever before me" (Isaiah 49:15-16).

19

THE SECRET LIFE of TREES

"Strange that so few ever come to the woods to see how the pine lives and grows and spires, lifting its evergreen arms to the light — to see its perfect success."
–Henry David Thoreau

Strange indeed. And sad. To miss the majesty of a tree is to miss one of the wonders of the world. Trees have been my salvation. As a child, I climbed trees to harvest their solitude. There, hidden from the cares of the world, cradled in an embryo of leafy greens, I whiled away the afternoon. I pondered. I imagined. I dreamed. My mother often claimed my head was in the clouds (or trees). Perhaps she was right. I was wonderstruck by the grandeur of a tree, as was Joyce Kilmer when he penned:

Trees

I think that I shall never see
A poem lovely as a tree.
A tree whose hungry mouth is prest
Against the earth's sweet flowing breast;
A tree that looks at God all day,
And lifts her leafy arms to pray;
A tree that may in summer wear
A nest of robins in her hair;
Upon whose bosom snow has lain;
Who intimately lives with rain.
Poems are made by fools like me,
But only God can make a tree.[1]

I wholeheartedly agree that only God can make a tree. But I must tell you that people are trying.

BBC News reports that Dr. Karl Lackner, a physicist at New York's

CROSS SECTION OF A TREE

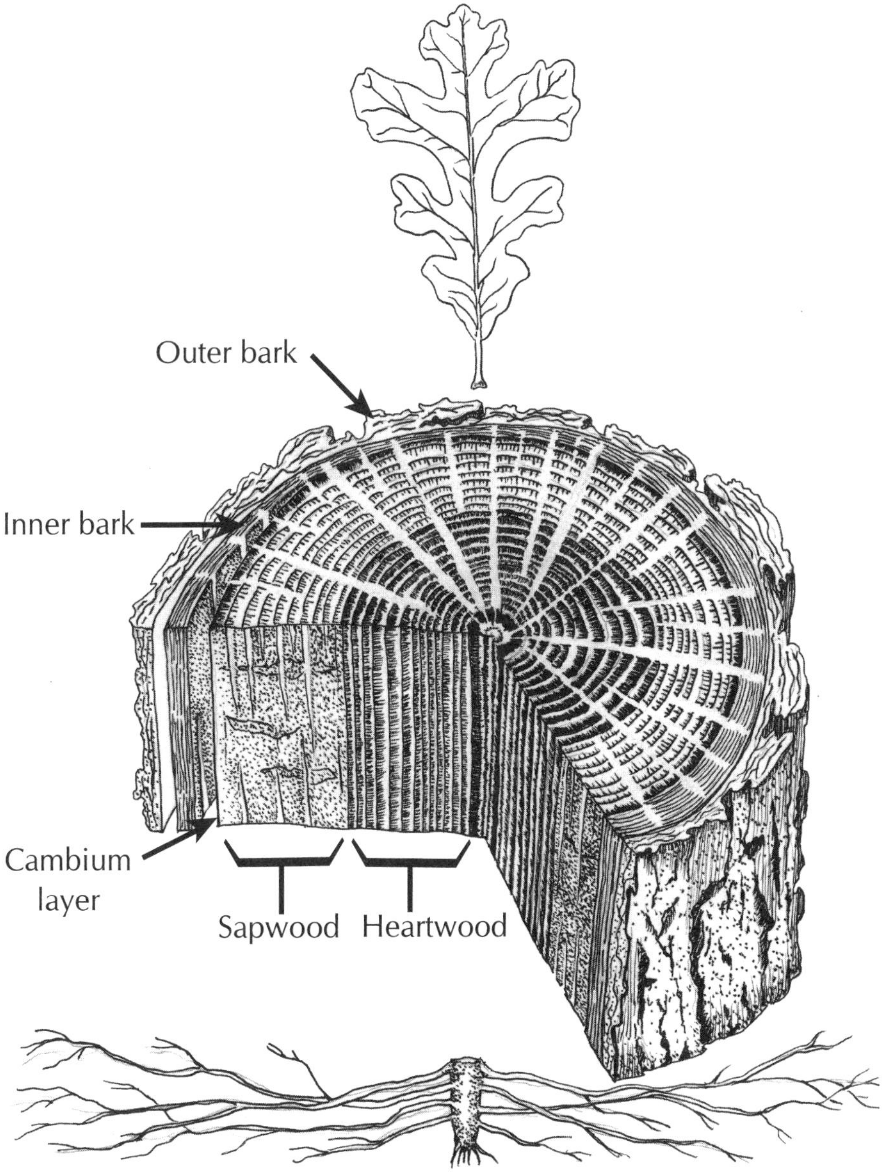

Columbia University has drafted plans for a synthetic tree—an artificial air filter of sorts. Lackner speculates that one synthetic tree could absorb ninety thousand tons of carbon dioxide a year, the equivalent to the exhaust emissions of fifteen thousand vehicles. If the idea is good, the design is ghastly. By his own admission, the imitation redwood "looks like a goal post with venetian blinds."[2] Humph.

If that weren't enough, *Scientific American* magazine tells of an entrepreneur's dream to develop a forest of fake trees which would have enough "juice" to electrify a city. Alex van der Beek, of the Netherlands, founder of the company Solar Botanic, is the proponent of the super tree which would "harvest sun and wind to generate electricity."[3] Each tree (twenty feet in diameter) is projected to cost between twelve thousand and twenty thousand dollars—it takes a lot of green to be green.

Not everyone is embracing this branch of new technology. Some are skeptical. Michael Woodhouse, a solar energy specialist from Golden, Colorado says,

> A lot of people are trying to catch the green energy wave, and sometimes it's half-baked science.[4]

Call me old fashioned, but I'll take the gnarled and knotted, strong and stately, God-made tree any day. Let's consider the wondrous ways of the tree as we peel back the layers and peer inside. If you could slice a slab of tree from its midsection and serve it up on a platter, you would notice an array of bands stacked vertically creating a triple layer cake of sorts. Each band plays a vital role in the life of the tree. Let's dissect that slice, one layer at a time.

BARK: The Outer Layer

Bark, the skin of the tree, is its protective covering. Bark consists of two layers of previously living cells. The outer bark is the "guard" layer, insulating the tree from injury, disease, and insect attack. The inner bark is a tree's version of a "meals on wheels" program, consisting of a series of linked tubes carrying food. Nutrients produced in the leaves are transferred down the trunk though the tube-like cells to the tips of its toes—the roots—and delivered everywhere in between. This inner bark transport system is called phloem tissue.

While I appreciate the aesthetic value of bark—the beauty of its color and texture—bark also carries economic value. At least two important everyday products hail from the bark of a tree: aspirin and cinnamon, my personal favorites, though not necessarily in that order.

Willow bark effectively reduces fever and inflammation. In the fifth century B.C. Greek physician Hippocrates is said to have used the bitter powder to treat such maladies. We now know that willow bark contains the natural compound salicylic acid—the precursor to synthetic aspirin.

Sandwiched somewhere between bark and Bayer in the history of aspirin, is the episode of an English pastor conducting "clinical trials" on the effect of willow bark on his parishioners. As a pastor's wife, I find this particularly fascinating. My husband has done some interesting things, but thankfully, testing the effects of medicinal herbs on parishioners is not among them.

In 1763 the Reverend Edward Stone conducted the first "official" scientific study of the compound and presented his findings in a letter to the Royal Society—kind of a who's who and what's what of science in England. Stone wrote,

> About six years ago, I accidentally tasted willow bark and was surprised at its extraordinary bitterness; which immediately raised me the suspicion of its having the properties of the Peruvian bark.[5]

How Stone "accidentally" tasted willow bark is a detail that intrigues me, but I must leave that tasty tidbit to my overactive imagination.

Stone was seeking a cure for malaria. At that time, treatment came primarily in the form of Peruvian cinchona bark, an expensive import. Walter Sneader, in his book *Drug Discovery*, notes that Stone also told the society that over the course of six years

> he had successfully treated fifty people with agues (malarial fevers) by giving them dried willow bark to consume

—clinical trials if you will.[6] However politically incorrect that may seem in light of today's medical laws, Stone's bark biting experiments ultimately yielded that bottle of Bayer you likely have in your medicine cabinet. His experiments were the precursor to the eventual isolation of the compound salicylic acid—now known as the key ingredient in the world's most popular drug: aspirin.

While willow bark extract is bitter and medicinal, the bark of the cinnamon tree is known for its ability to stir up warm memories in recesses of our minds. Tilt your head heavenward, breathe deep and imagine the scent of cinnamon wafting through the air. Your thoughts? If you're like most of us, you are transported back in time to a happy memory. Sense of smell can do that. According to Rachel Herz, author of *Scent of Desire*, the sense of smell is

> integrally tied to our emotions, our memories, our behaviors and our health. Scents influence our social relationships and family ties, and they fuel our passions for people and food.[7]

It is safe to say that scent affects our sense of well-being.

Perhaps this is why we love our cinnamon. Second only to black pepper, cinnamon is the runner-up spice in the race of spices sold in U.S. and European markets. What you may not know is that there are various species of trees that satisfy our cinnamon craving, the most popular being true cinnamon, which hails from the *Cinnamomum verum* tree, and cassia cinnamon, from the *Cinnamomum cassia* tree. It takes a discriminating palate to distinguish between the two, but the experts tell us that true cinnamon has a more delicate flavor, with cassia cinnamon being more pungent. Overall, the two are used interchangeably. And in Exodus chapter 30, both are listed as important spices.

Cinnamon, from either tree, is harvested from the inner bark. The harvesting method varies depending upon the country of harvest, but the basic method involves stripping the outer bark from the tree or branches. Next, the inner bark is shaved off in long strips. Upon drying, the moist bark curls up into quills, those rolled rounds of cinnamon we call "cinnamon sticks."

SAPWOOD: The Middle Layer

Next to the inner bark lies the sapwood. This layer is responsible for a tree's growth in circumference or girth. Trees have two types of growth: up and out, or primary and secondary growth. Primary growth of the tree increases the height and length of the tree. Secondary growth increases the girth of the tree and occurs in the middle layer of our vertical tree "cake." The microscopic cambium layer, a thin, frosting-like band of goodness, is responsible for expanding the girth of the tree. Another sweet miracle in God's bakery of creation.

If the bark is akin to skin, the cambium layer could be considered the marrow of the tree, producing living cells necessary for trees to survive. Just as the bone marrow produces life giving blood cells, the cambium layer produces a layer of delicate tree tissue responsible for delivering essential nutrients fluidly throughout the tree. Phloem (think food) transports nutrients produced in the leaves downward distributing the goods throughout the tree, while the xylem moves water and other essential fluids in the opposite direction-up from the roots. This thin frosting-like layer flows freely at first. Eventually, however, over time this "frosting layer" hardens, creating a cellular traffic jam, and the lanes clog up. The cells can no longer function in transport and instead become heartwood.

HEARTWOOD: The Strength of a Tree

Wood is transformed into heartwood as the xylem and phloem cells mature and succumb to the wear and tear of life, preventing fluid transport. Over time, this process produces the dark central core you see in the stump of a tree. This central core, and the cambium layer which is continually producing new cells, combine together to form the annual rings of the tree. Heartwood is a "historical museum" displaying a record of the years gone by, preserved in its rings. Heartwood—a fitting name for a wood that preserves history and provides strength and structure to the tree—truly is the heart of the tree.

ROOTS: The Anchor

I would be remiss if I neglected to mention the root of the tree. The root, though unseen, plays an integral role in the life of the tree and deserves a shout out. For under every standing sentinel grows the humble root. Without its roots, the tree is nothing more than a pile of nutrient starved, dried up timber. Roots literally ground and anchor the plant, in addition to providing the necessary water and minerals they extract from the soil.

Tucked within the secret lives of trees are valuable lessons for our own lives. The layers of the tree parallel the layers of happiness and joy in life. Just as the bark of a tree is its superficial, outer layer, happiness is fleeting and can be peeled from our lives in seconds—just look at Job. Our joy must come from something which lasts, not the rapidly changing circumstances of our lives. Dwight L. Moody once said,

> Happiness is caused by the things that happen around me, and circumstances will mar it; but joy flows right on through trouble; joy flows on through the dark; joy flows in the night as well as in the day; joy flows all through persecution and opposition. It is an unceasing fountain bubbling up in the heart; a secret weapon the world can't see and doesn't know anything about.[8]

The source of joy lies deep in our souls, beneath the outer bark of our lives and penetrates into the inner sanctum of our hearts. Tucked within our core is the living layer of Christ. Though we may experience pain and trials that beat on the surface of our lives, lodged deep within is the penetrating peace of Christ—our "cambium layer," generating new life in our tired and battered soul cells. His power renews. His power restores. Over time, he builds conduits of joy within our soul.

And just as the roots are the anchor and source of water for a tree, so Christ grounds and refreshes us.

> So then, just as you received Christ Jesus as Lord, continue to live in him rooted and built up in him, strengthened in the faith as you were taught, and overflowing with thankfulness.[9]

We need only to be rooted in him. Dig deep, my friend!

WONDERCISE

Tree Time

Spending time with trees can shape our perspective on life. As a child I spent endless hours in my tree house. Built in the boughs of a sturdy nectarine tree, "Tree" and I shared the seasons of life. I grew hopeful in spring when the growth of buds appeared, restful in summer under her emerald umbrella, wistful in fall and winter for spring's return. Some forty years later, I still enjoy time in the company of a tree.

You, too, can enrich your life by observing a tree through the seasons.

Knapsack Needs:

- Hand lens
- Binoculars (optional)
- Camera (optional)

Select a nearby tree from your surroundings—in your yard, neighborhood, or park—close enough to visit once a month. Become a student of this tree.

On your initial visit, as you settle into this tree time, quiet your mind and engage your senses. Describe the tree and its surroundings and enter your findings in your notebook:

Shape: Is the tree compact, with its branches close to its trunk (slim-line), or broad and wide with spreading branches (lollipop-style)?

Leaf type: Are the leaves round, oval, or heart-shaped? Small or large? Soft and smooth? Tough and leathery? Are the leaf edges lobed, toothed, or smooth?

Bark and Blossoms: Note the type and texture of the bark. Is the tree in blossom? Does it have fruit or seeds?

Community: Who goes there? Use your hand lens and look for tiny dwellers in and on the bark.

Branch dwellers: Use your binoculars to look for signs of nests.

With each subsequent visit, record the general appearance of the tree, noting any changes. Over the course of the year, you may notice the tree's "firsts"—first leaves, first flower, first signs of leaf fall, etc.

My hope is that as you observe this tree through the rhythm of the seasons, you will take note of any seasons of growth, abundance, and rest in your own life. God can teach us much if we open our hearts, minds, and eyes to the world around us, even through the life of one solitary tree.

Promise of Hope

"But blessed is the man who trusts in the Lord, whose confidence is in him, He will be like a tree planted by the water that sends out its roots by the stream. It does not fear when heat comes; its leaves are always green. It has no worries in a year of drought and never fails to bear fruit" (Jeremiah 17:7-8).

PART V
Gifts of the Desert

"The best gift of the desert is God's presence."
–Paul E. Miller

20
Of TOADS and TRIALS

"In His time, in His way, He will turn my dryness into a river of love.
-David Wilkerson

I confess. Occasionally I experience "stress-tivation"—a self-coined word originating from the scientific term *estivation*. Estivation is just a fancy term for the summer equivalent of hibernation, when animals withdraw from harsh environmental conditions. "Stress-tivation" describes my response to difficult situations. When life's conditions get too hot to handle, I retreat. Spiritually dehydrated and discouraged, I dive as deeply away from stress as I can. Basically, I am no better than a spadefoot toad. When faced with the unbearable arid conditions of the desert, the spadefoot digs into the sand where it remains for nine to ten months and awaits the return of the life-giving rains.

If a toad in the desert strikes you like a fish out of water, you're not alone. People are often surprised to learn that toads and frogs inhabit dry grasslands and deserts. Yet the spadefoot toad carves out quite a life for himself in the desert sands. The secret to his success depends on his ability to go underground—made possible by a Swiss-army-knife-like gadget tucked between his toes.

I'm a gadget lover. Christmastime gives me an excuse to buy them—from the raisin-pooping reindeer dispenser to electrified socks, I seek out crazy gadgets. The more unusual the better.

The spadefoot toad has a gadget of his own stuffed in his stocking. Just look at his hind foot. So unusual is this foot, the genus was named for it. Biologist Dr. Arthur Bragg says of the spadefoot, "The hind feet are markedly webbed like those of a frog … in the ankle region of each leg, a dark prominence with a sharp cutting edge occurs."[1] Using that sharp spade, the toad sinks into the soil, deftly digging himself a cave in the desert to depths of up to three feet.

SPADE FOOT TOAD
(*Scaphiopus couchii*)

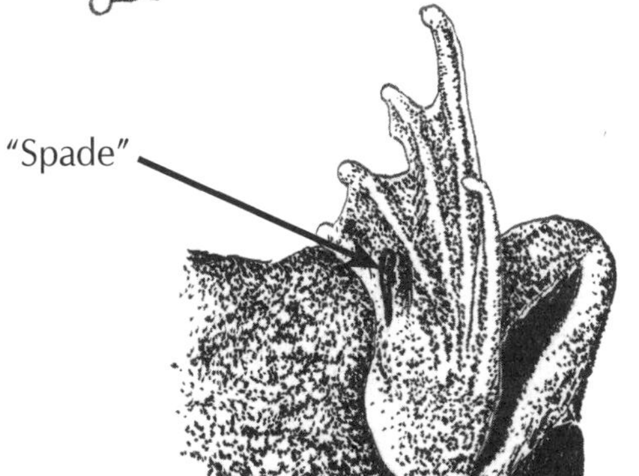

Hind Foot With Digging Spade

Spade Foot Digging Into The Desert Sands

In addition to getting down and dirty, the spadefoot has some internal tricks in its arsenal. When entering estivation, the toad must adapt to a life of stillness and endure long periods without food or water. Life in the burrow requires drastic water and energy conservation measures. Water problems are solved by osmosis. Osmosis is simply the movement of molecules from an area of higher concentration into an area of lesser concentration—similar to how the scent molecules of chocolate chip cookies fresh out of the oven spread throughout the house. That's osmosis. As a child, I remember putting a math book under my pillow hoping knowledge would seep into my head as I slept. A wishful osmosis of sorts. No such luck.

Fortunately for the spadefoot, osmosis works—in a weird and wonderful way. This toad has the ability to retain bladder urine which results in body fluids with higher concentrations of urea than water. This is actually a good thing for a toad. Due to the law of osmosis, because the water in the soil is greater than the water in the toad, water flows into the toad via its permeable skin. Simply by being in contact with the soil, the toad absorbs water. A nifty arrangement, to be sure.

After spending nearly a year in the pit, the spadefoot awaits the rains. The exact trigger for emergence is unknown, but these toads are said to emerge by the thousands. Overnight the desert floor can be transformed into a tapestry of toads. Scientists believe that they have a vibration detection system that tips them off.

Sort of a Snow White of the sands, the sleeping spadefoot is awakened by the kiss of rain upon the ground. This awakening gives way to frenzied digging to the surface, where the search for a mate begins. No time to be selective, the spadefoot must breed immediately, so that the eggs (a female can lay up to three thousand eggs) can hatch and reach toadhood before the ponds dry up and leave the newbie high and dry. The eggs are said to hatch only nine hours after being laid, with the tadpole to toad cycle completed in as little as ten days. Time is of the essence. For when the rains recede the ephemeral ponds will fade away. By September the toads are digging in again. The spadefoot life cycle—egg, tadpole, toadlet, adult—when divided into stages, finds the toad spending the majority of its lifetime in a cave. This retreat to the cave is a protective, life-saving measure.

Now, I must tell you, cave retreats are biblical. Elijah experienced his own case of stress-tivation and sought refuge in a cave. What drove him to the cave occurred after the supernatural, fire-from-heaven miracle of 1 Kings chapter 18. Initially, the miracle fired Elijah up. God had trumped Baal by consuming the sacrifice with holy fire. And the people on the sidelines "fell prostrate and cried, 'The LORD—he is God!'" On the heels of this miracle came another. Rains returned and ended the drought. So energized was he by this success, Elijah ran past King Ahab riding in his chariot and beat him back to the land of the castle. Elijah was certain this event would inspire Ahab to a change of heart and all would live "happily ever after." He expected it. Imagine his shock when Ahab's "Elijah Report" to Jezebel generated not thunderous applause but vitriolic death threats. Tucking his fears and his failures in his belt, Elijah ran for cover.

How often our expectations disappoint us. Detailed are the expectations we create in vivid, living color. Yet, when the scene actually plays out it debuts in black and white, act two is missing, and the ending has been rewritten. That's God. He knows the scenes of our lives. He calls the shots and directs the plays.

God does not have to prove himself. Ever. We may have expectations and imagine an event will turn out just so; but that is our plan, not God's. Recently, I had the audacity to tell God that he had the opportunity to redeem himself by healing my mom of cancer. Here was his chance to make up for the cancer that killed my dad forty years earlier. Mind you, I am not in the habit of challenging God to a spiritual dual, and don't recommend it, but I dealt with my pain by putting God to a dare. This was my foolhardy plan. I fully expected God to redeem himself by healing my mom. My, my, my … my way. My plan. My arrogance.

Elijah also had a problem with personal expectations. It led him into trouble just as my expectations tripped me up. Frustrated and afraid, Elijah ran away and fumed under a broom tree. He had had enough. Elijah mistakenly believed he had failed. Tired and discouraged, he couldn't go on. Yet in Elijah's weakest moment, God provided an angel to care for him. (I don't ever recall receiving an angelic appearance during my desperate days, but then I'm not Elijah.) After the angel's touch, Elijah wandered in the wilderness. Forty days and forty nights later Elijah sought the refuge of a cave. Not the refuge of God, mind you, but the refuge of a cave.

There in the cave, God showed up with a pertinent question: "What are you doing here, Elijah?" (I Kings 19:9). Such an interesting choice of words. God was asking Elijah, "What's up?" You see, God knew his heart. God knew the disappointment and discouragement Elijah felt in the failure to effect change in Jezebel. But Elijah just didn't get it. He was clueless as to the plan of God and was blinded by his own expectations.

God's question was more of a personal probe, going deeper, and penetrating his soul. Similar to what the monastic desert fathers experienced when they sought refuge in the cave of the wilderness. Monastic cells, often nothing more than a cramped and chilly dugout cave, provided shelter from the elements and from life's distractions. Monks craved the cave of contemplation. Mind you, there are times when self-examination is necessary. However, there comes a time when self-examination becomes self-serving.

Sometimes our spiritual caves can become our refuge instead of God. Sometimes we run to our cave instead of running to God. God, however, brings us to our senses. Jonah uttered these words from the smelly belly of the whale cave:

> To the roots of the mountains I sank down; the earth barred me in forever. But you brought my life up from the pit, O Lord my God (Jonah 2:6).

And God also brought Elijah to his senses in the cave. God told Elijah, "Go back." Twice. When the cave becomes too embryonic, too comfortable, too safe, God calls us out. Sometimes the answer to our problems comes when we return to them and face them head on. With God.

Yet sometimes it is too painful to push through the soil of life's problems. I want to avoid the pain. I'd really rather be a toad. It's easier. When overwhelmed by life's problems and I have flunked the faith test, I tend to bury myself in the sands of solitude. I long to live the hermit lifestyle of the desert fathers, who sought to escape the evils of life by embracing the solitude of the cave. I take comfort in the fact that cave dwelling Elijah is described as "a man like us" (James 5:17). Elijah ran from reality and I can relate. Yet it is precisely during those dry spells of life when we enter the wilderness that we come face to face with God. And ourselves.

Days in the wilderness yield new discoveries. Consider the life of Darius Nash Couch. Couch was an officer in the U.S. Army. For reasons unknown, Couch ventured from routine to seek adventure in the wilderness. Taking a year's leave of absence, he conducted a scientific expedition to Mexico in 1853 for the benefit of the Smithsonian Institution. Couch risked the comforts of the home cave for discovery in the desert. Letters document a portion of his adventure:

> With two pack mules & two mounted servants I crossed the River at Brownsville and struck west towards Monterey, the Capital of Nuevo Leon—travelling at slow marches in order to gather information of the Country, its people, and fill my panniers with specimens in Natural History etc.[2]

And on that journey, Couch discovered the toad that came to be named Couch's spadefoot toad (*Scaphiopus couchii*) in his honor. This was a discovery that would forever etch Couch's name in history.

How about us? Will we endure hardship to follow God? Will we step out of the comfort of our cave and seek adventure for God? The journey is difficult, but the rewards are great. And our names will also be written down in the book of life. Forever. Now that's a reward worth seeking.

WONDERCISE

Spring Sing

Spring sings with the sounds of toads and frogs. That symphony can function as an advertisement to attract mates or as an alarm to startle predators. The basic call is produced when a frog or toad fills its vocal sac and lungs with air. That air is then forced over the vocal chords; the sac inflates and produces drum-like vibrations. Each species has its own unique voice.

Knapsack Needs:

- Field guide to amphibians
- Flashlight

To hear their call, take a trip to the desert's vernal ponds during the season of spring rains—or visit a local wetland.

Listen: Just after sundown, select a suitable potential frog or toad habitat. Spend some time listening for their calls, which can range from flute-like melodies to deep drum-like beats.

Look: Frogs often sit in the vegetation at the edge of ponds. Slowly walk around the water's edge and keep your eyes peeled for their quick movement.

Learn: In many areas, frog populations are on the decline. Many states have active amphibian monitoring programs. Check for one of these programs in your area and volunteer to lend an ear and learn about amphibians in your area.

Frogs aren't the only ones that will benefit from this time well spent. Relax as you contemplate the creature that lives in rhythm with the seasons.

Promise of Hope

"He brought me out into a spacious place; he rescued me because he delighted in me" (Psalm 18:19).

21

THE RESURRECTION PLANT
Roll Up and Dry

"The LORD will fight for you; you need only to be still. Then the LORD said to Moses, Why are you crying out to me? Tell the Israelites to move on."
Exodus 14:14-15

How do you know when it's time to move on? And which direction should you go? This is where I often fail. I pray in earnest, yet the answer eludes me. Indecision paralyzes me. One time while driving Ireland's rural roads, I came to a multi-tined fork in the road. The intersection diverged into six branching roads. The road sign boasted a quiver of directional arrows mounted on a pole, each pointing a different direction. One destination even had two arrows—one faced east, the other west. Confusion reigned. Unsure how to proceed, I sat rooted in the middle of the road.

Seems Moses and his people, in Exodus chapter 14, came up against something like that Irish road sign. In verse 14 Moses tells his people to chill and be still—the road sign reads a tenth of a mile to relaxation (O'Casey translation). Just as they slow their donkey to a stopping point, God shouts "Giddyup! Stop whining, get up, and move on" (verse 15, O'Casey translation continued). So which is it? Be still or move on? Life throws us curves and challenges. Sometimes we must be still; other times we must move.

Maybe that's why I am fond of the resurrection plant—it has both the fight and flight gene. While rooted, this rough and tumble weed of sorts endures the heat using a couple of physiological tricks it has tucked up its stem. Yet in true nomadic fashion, the plant can roll out when things get too hot to handle and wander on the whisper of the wind. For a plant, this is remarkable. And unusual.

THE RESURRECTION PLANT (Selaginella lepidophylla)

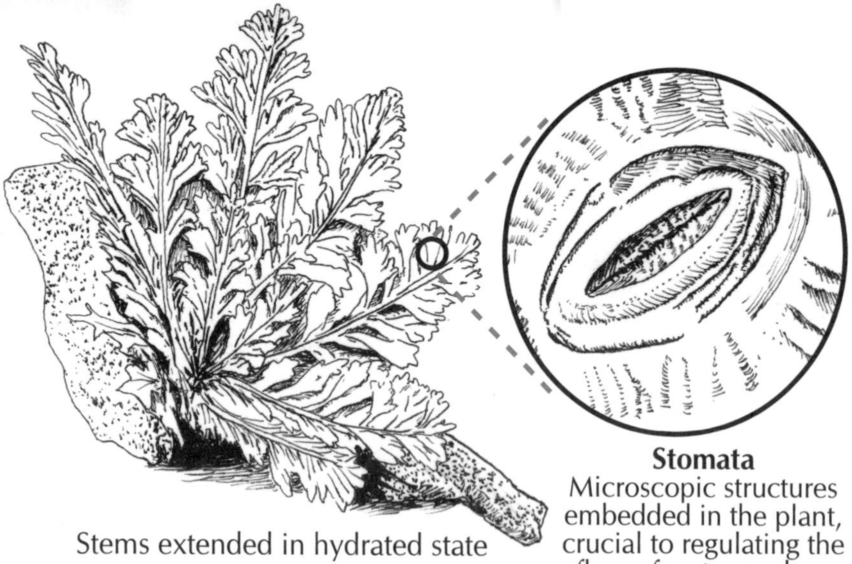

Stems extended in hydrated state

Stomata
Microscopic structures embedded in the plant, crucial to regulating the flow of water, carbon dioxide and oxygen

Stems retracted in dessicated state

Most plants as we know them are just that—planted. Rooted. Grounded. Coping with harsh climate conditions when you can't move is tricky. Yet some plants, called xerophytes, require little water and are built to withstand heat by employing one of two strategies: evade or endure.

- **The Evader**: Turn up the heat, banish the beverage and the plant shuts down. The annual is such a plant. It is as though this plant sticks its stem in the arid air and says, "Fine, I will just live life in the good times, when water is plentiful. I will sprout, leaf out, flower, seed, and die—all before the wretched heat arrives. And my seed will endure." When the rains come, the cycle begins again. The California poppy is a classic example of an evader plant.

- **The Endurer**: Plants in this class seek not to escape the heat, but stand in the face of dehydration. One such plant is the resurrection plant, the common name given to several varieties of plants in arid regions named for their ability to "resurrect" from the dead. To come back to life. This plant is endowed with physiological features which enable it to tough it out, curl up, and die … er … dry. Then, like a sponge, when soaked in water the plant springs back to life.

In addition, the resurrection plant can also move out and ride the whispers of the wind. *Plants of the Bible*, a book considered to be the standard reference on biblical botany, suggests that the rolling plant referred to in Psalm 83:13 and Isaiah 17:13 is the Palestinian tumbleweed (*Anastatica hierochuntica)*, a "typical tumbleweed and resurrection plant."[1] This Mediterranean plant with its tiny puckered leaves is a member of the mustard family and its twelve-inch circular globe of a skeleton roams the land where Jesus walked.

The American version of the resurrection plant, called the rose of Jericho (*Selaginella lepidophylla*), is a different beast altogether, closer in kind to mosses and ferns. While researching, I discovered a bargain basement website that advertised the resurrection plant as a "prehistoric evergreen that just won't die" for only $7.99. Ironically, it's listed under "science toys" and is certainly something I would have saved my nickels for as a child. The small round ball of faux moss literally comes to life in water. Interestingly, the part that we call a leaf is actually an extension of the stem and you won't find a flower on it, for it reproduces by spores. I think Geek.com nails it when it tags this plant as "one of a kind."

The resurrection plant is legendary. According to one story, when Jesus withdrew to the desert to pray, the resurrection plant, moist with dew from the night, unfurled its branches and offered its precious moisture to the Lord. Jesus took the drops of refreshment to his parched lips and was blessed. Another story says the Spanish friars of the new world used the plant to demonstrate the concept of rebirth in the Christian faith.

My husband often uses the rose of Jericho plant to illustrate the hope of the resurrection in the face of death. At the beginning of a funeral he unveils the dry and withered plant. He immerses it into a bowl of clear water. He then preaches the eulogy. Near the end of the service, the plant has begun to show signs of life. Resurrection demonstrated. Hope restored.

Just how does this plant come to life again? Endowed with some unique structures and abilities in the form of stomata, sugars, and "stretchy" proteins, the resurrection plant pulls off this amazing stunt. Check it out.

Leaves are a plant's Achilles' heel, as it were. Crucial to the life of the plant, leaves function as food factories, yet they need a way to exchange oxygen and carbon dioxide without succumbing to life-threatening water loss. Leaves come equipped with tiny adjustable valves to regulate the flow of gases and water. Looking like little pairs of lips, these microscopic valves are tucked on the underside of leaves and are called stomata, a Greek word that means mouth or a mouth-like opening.

Imagine a tiny sliding glass door of sorts embedded in the leaf. When the door is closed, no moisture loss occurs. That's a good thing. However, with the door closed, food production shuts down as carbon dioxide cannot enter. In xerophytic plants, the hours of food production have been altered to better suit the life of the plant. These plants work the graveyard shift long after the sun goes down.

Using a process called CAM photosynthesis (over achievers can look up the details), the resurrection plant thinks "outside the leaf." While most plants shut their stomas at night and conduct food production operations in daylight hours, the resurrection plant does just the opposite. The food factory stays open all night, when temperatures are cooler, and humidity levels higher. The plant converts the carbon dioxide into an acid and stores it overnight for use the next day to complete photosynthesis. The system works like a well-oiled machine and is crucial for survival in the desert heat. Such details are the work of a heavenly engineer.

Another product necessary for food processing is sugar. And as the old saying goes, just a spoonful of sugar helps the medicine go down, or in this case, relieves stress. I really didn't need scientific journals to tell me this. I am a firm proponent of sweets during times of crises. It would seem that the resurrection plant has the same philosophy.

Shoot a little sugar in its veins, and the plant breathes a sigh of relief. But not just any sugar. The sugary stress relief comes from a naturally occurring sugar called trehalose, which is found in a variety of organisms such as invertebrates, fungi, and bacteria, but typically is found in plants in trace amounts. One exception is the mighty resurrection plant.

Studies have shown the resurrection plant accumulates trehalose at levels up to twelve percent of its body weight during dehydration. *Science Daily* shares a quote from Cornell molecular plant biologist Ajay Garg on the wonder of trehalose in the resurrection plant:

> Drought stressed resurrection plants look like they are dead and gone forever; then they pop back to life when moisture is available. That's the power of trehalose in combating stress, and it gave us an idea to help important crop plants survive stress.[2]

Drought dramatically threatens the world's food supply. Imagine if rice plants could be more drought tolerant. Scientists experimenting with genes and needles (don't try this at home) found that trehalose accumulation in rice plants confers high tolerance to desiccation. This could expand the cultivation possibilities of rice worldwide.

And all this came from observing the ability of the resurrection plant to shrivel up and survive. The fact that the resurrection plant can dry without shattering brings me to another remarkable factor of its physiology: it's a "stretchy" plant. The cell walls of this plant shrink, and it curls up and dries. This is one thing. But to "un-shrink" is another thing altogether. The resurrection plant can swell and shrink indefinitely. Repeatedly. How does it do this? In another species of resurrection plant (*Craterostigma plantagineum*), scientists discovered that one component required for the stretch factor is a class of proteins that provide the plant an "uncommon degree" of wall flexibility.[3] These cell wall modifying proteins, called "expansins," allow it more flexibility than a yogi master.

Proteins are not just for muscle building. Sometimes they are for cell wall folding. Flexibility is the key to surviving life in a dry and thirsty world.

The resurrection plant toughs it out in times of drought—with its strength in stillness. But remember, I said that this plant can also pull up stakes and move out. It can cut and run. Literally. And trigger the tumble factor. The resurrection plant is able to disconnect from its roots and tumble onward in the wind, bringing new meaning to "cut your losses and move on."

How do we respond to difficult situations? Are we of the "fight or flight" mentality? Do we endure or evade? Personally, the evasion method fails me every time. When I employ the "rip and roll" maneuver, I find the same situation waiting for me to deal with upon arrival in the new location. Maybe the faces have changed but the problem remains the same. I have learned I must endure and deal with the problem, not evade the situation.

Dry times rarely find me dancing for joy. I do, however, gain a new perspective on endurance. Despite my desire to run, I find that in putting down roots and planting my feet firmly on the ground, I learn trust. My Father teaches me that despite the winds and the drought, he will see me through. I may be battered, I may be withered, but I will survive. I toughen my thin, tomato skin hide and wait for the rain. For I know that the water of life will once again course through my thirsty spiritual veins and resurrect my soul.

WONDERCISE

Dehydration Divas of the Desert

Survival in the desert requires the right stuff. Many desert plants are uniquely built to survive dry times. See if you can notice the difference.

Knapsack Needs:

- Hand lens
- Field guide to desert plants

Take a trip to the desert, or visit a garden center and observe the plants in the xerophyte section. Study their leaves—shape, size, and texture. How do the leaves differ?

- Are the leaves large or small? Smaller leaves mean less exposure to sun.
- Are the leaves waxy or resinous? Wax helps to reduce water evaporation.
- Are the leaves smooth, or covered with spines or fine hairs? These structures aid the plant in heat reflection.

Consider the variety in leaf types as God's protection system for plants. In his creative genius, he has given both plants and humans the ability to survive life in the desert.

Promise of Hope

"We were therefore buried with him through baptism into death in order that, just as Christ was raised from the dead through the glory of the Father, we too may live a new life" (Romans 6:4).

22
SHOREBIRDS in the DESERT

"Life is a journey, not a destination."
–Ralph Waldo Emerson

The romance began under the frigid, mist-infused skies of "avian" Route 66 (the Pacific Flyway) in Willapa Bay, Washington. It was love at first flight. Call it an on-the-job affair if you will. My assignment to monitor the fitness of migrating shorebirds both excited and terrified me. I was excited to witness shorebirds eleven days into their journey, yet terrified to take the fragile feathered lives in my hands.

My chilled fingers barely functioned as I removed the tiny bundle of bird from the net. The rapid pulse of her heart mirrored my own and I contrasted the immensity of her journey with the minuteness of her mass. I measured her vitals. How could a mere 1.6 ounces of feather, beak and bone venture thousands of miles? Physically, it seemed impossible. Yet straining against my trembling fingers lay proof—a petite stick of pure avian dynamite. In reverent silence, I opened the palm of my hand. She took to the skies and never looked back, the beat of her wings echoing the poignant words of Robert Frost, "I have promises to keep, and miles to go before I sleep …"[1]

That day stands forever etched in my memory. For on that day I saw my own life's journey illustrated in the mural of the migratory shorebird's life.

Migration has intrigued humans for centuries. Even the pages of the Bible flutter with the seasonal wonders of migration. "Even the stork in the sky knows her appointed seasons, and the dove, the swift, and the thrush observe the time of their migration" (Jeremiah 8:7).

The word migration hails from the Latin *migrare*, which means "to go from one place to another." While many animals migrate, the record for the longest documented round trip belongs to a bird. The Sooty

SEMIPALMATED PLOVER
(Charadrius semipalmatus)

Shearwater holds the prize for completing a journey of 39,790 miles in 262 days. As such, shorebirds have earned the title "champion migrators." Twice a year, spring and fall, the salty winged travelers fill the skies by the thousands, navigating invisible highways. But before they take to the skies, they engage in some pre-flight preparation.

Preparation for the journey is critical. They cram for migration finals. Literally. Not with knowledge, but with food. Pre-migration, shorebirds commit hyperphagy. If we break the word into its Greek roots, we find that *hyper* means "over," and *phag* means "food." Hyperphagy is a fancy way to say over-eat. I love this word. It describes my ice cream and cookie binges in a socially acceptable way. Unlike my hyperphagous events, however, shorebirds commit hyperphagy for a reason other than stress relief. Shorebirds plunge their beaks into the sand with the gusto of an oil derrick on crack and stuff themselves with food for preflight fueling. And they pack on the pounds (or ounces). Shorebirds consume an additional fifty percent of their body weight before liftoff.

Even birds, however, are not immune to weight problems. In an intriguing research paper I would have loved to call "Too Fat to Fly" (hence I write for the general public, and not for scientific journals if I can help it) researcher Joseph R. Jehl, Jr. found that overindulgence can be a show stopper for migrating birds. Jehl discovered that small shorebirds, called Wilson's Phalaropes, that overate and packed fat to the tune of fifty four percent of their body weight were temporarily grounded—literally.[2] It seems that too much of a good thing can be a deterrent to lift off. Fat birds don't fly. Who knew?

In another study on an equally intriguing topic concerning shorebirds and performance enhancing substances, researchers investigated the role of dietary fats in the migration of the Semipalmated Sandpiper.[3] It seems that not only the amount of food ingested, but the type of food plays a role in performance. This sandpiper species performs an enormously long-distance migration, a transoceanic, nonstop journey of 4500 km in three days. To bulk up for the trip, the bird engages in a preflight eating orgy that involves two weeks of gorging on a small shrimp-like animal rich in polyunsaturated fatty acids (PUFA). Research shows that long-distance migrant birds can use natural diets rich in PUFA to prime their flight muscles for endurance exercise—a handy feat. PUFA benefits are not just for the birds and are believed to improve aerobic performances and provide beneficial health effects in humans.

Okay, so with PUFA power on board and the extra ounces packed away, the bird is primed for takeoff. The journey begins. Fuel costs are expensive, however, and eventually its gage reads empty. Birds descend from on high and camp along the way. Well, sort of. Camping for me is a time of rest—and gorging. I consume too many calories in the form of s'mores and M&M trail mix. For migrating birds, however, camping is not a frivolous luxury, but essential to survival. They need to rest and refuel for the long haul.

Recently, my son and daughter-in-law hiked the John Muir trail—all 211 miles of it. Like birds, they carried everything they needed on their backs. And, like birds, when they exhausted their food supply they replenished their fat stores—in a pizza joint. Shorebirds do this sans pizza, of course. They prefer polychaetes—nice juicy worms—and they know just the place to grab a bite.

Shorebirds frequent polychaete "diners" in the desert. That's right, if you see shorebirds in the desert, it may not be a mirage. Surprisingly, deserts can be a place of refuge on the journey. Despite all the pre-flight planning, the stores of fat eventually run thin and need to be replenished. Hence, into each shorebird's life a little desert must fall. On the Pacific Flyway, one such stop is in the middle of the Colorado Desert—the Salton Sea. The good news is that, despite the dry and dusty land, there is an oasis of sorts—the largest lake in California filled with good things for birds to eat. Shorebirds depend on these widely spaced pit stops to rest and refuel on their semi-annual migrations. Another desert stopover site, the Great Salt Lake, was dubbed the number one stopover site with 380,000 shorebird users—smack dab in the middle of dry ground. That's a lot of feet touching down in a dry and thirsty land.

Stopover sites have been analyzed for food content in several studies. Speaking from experience, I have been knee deep in Willapa Bay mud dredging up "bird dinner." The soupy mud yields a smorgasbord of entrees: invertebrate delicacies of worms, insect larvae, baby shrimp, crustaceans, and clams. And shorebirds indulge.

So they refuel, rest, and hop back on the aerial interstate and head north. Sounds easy, right? One thing we've neglected to mention is the navigational map. How do they know the way? I, myself, am directionally challenged. Once on an interstate journey with my friend Eva, I made a serious wrong turn. Running low on petrol, I pulled off the highway to refuel. Engaged in our usual incessant conversation, I rejoined the freeway (going the wrong direction) and drove onward, talking all the while.

Forty-five minutes later I noticed a sign that said Portland … ninety miles. *Humph*, I thought, *that's strange. We left Portland hours ago*. I looked at Eva. She looked at me. We erupted in laughter and changed our direction of travel. Obviously, I am not known for my directional skills. Birds are. How do they do it?

For starters, let's look at the elitist in GPS skills—the humble homing pigeon. This bird flies home despite all odds with impeccable navigation skills. They seem to be the guinea pigs in bird migration research. In the Cadillac of all experiments, a German researcher named Hans Wallraff tried to confuse the homing pigeon so it would not know the way home.

Wallraff hauled a bunch of homing pigeons to a distant location, placed them in an airtight, scent-proof, light-regulated, noise-jammed container which was surrounded by magnetic coils that caused a constantly changing magnetic field. The whole shebang rotated on a pedestal like the moon on steroids (yes, I know, we research types are an odd bunch). Could I find my way home after this? Not a chance. However, the homing pigeons were unaffected by the chaos. When released, the birds still found their way home. Seems the homing pigeon is unflappable. Based on pigeon games such as this, scientists speculate that birds have both an internal compass and internal map. Clearly something is going on.

Currently there are five prevailing theories of flight navigation: Sun Compass, Star Compass, Odor Map, Magnetic Map, Magnetic Compass—in no particular order of popularity. The debate rages on, as it has for years. Journals are full of conflicting information. One biologist sums it up with what I call the "birder GPS combo." Dr. Robert Beason, of the University of Louisiana, told the *New York Times* that "birds were generally thought to use multiple orientation cues, with the ability to reject one or other types of cue if needed."[4] Different methods for different migrants.

As I watch shorebirds touch down in the bay during migration, I am reminded of Psalm 84:

> Blessed are those whose strength is in you, who have set their hearts on pilgrimage. As they pass through the Valley of Baca, they make it a place of springs; the autumn rains also cover it with pools. They go from strength to strength, till each appears before God in Zion.

On this earth, are we not on a pilgrimage? As C. S. Lewis said,

> Our Father refreshes us on the journey with some pleasant inns, but will not encourage us to mistake them for home.[5]

We are just passing through—pilgrims in a dry and thirsty land—like shorebirds en route. And pilgrims encounter harsh lands on their journey. We would do well to remember the words of author John Ortberg:

> He is the God who takes his people to the Promised Land by way of the desert.[6]

Pilgrims don't, however, wander deserts aimlessly. Pilgrims travel with purpose. As such, we need to keep our eyes on the finish line, as runners in a race.

And be mindful of our inner compass. And above all, we must remember our final stomping grounds, for this earth is not our home. Life is a journey, not a destination. Oh that we could learn to enjoy the flight. God has planned it and ordained it after all. He guides; he provides.

We are pilgrims en route. Heaven is the destination. Migration is our journey. Let's remember to take time to rest and refuel, then resume the flight.

WONDERCISE

Seasonal Surprises

Be on the alert for seasonal surprises in the form of a visit from a traveling songster. Spring and fall yield migrants on the move. And because the birds don't read the guide books, you may be treated to a rare visitor. But in order to recognize this stranger, you must familiarize yourself with the regular customers.

Knapsack Needs:

- Binoculars
- Field guide to birds
- Bird feeder
- Bird seed
- Patience

Start feeding the regulars; then watch and observe. As you become familiar with the crowd, some birds will stand out as residents, which remain all year. Others are just passing through. These migrants jolt us from our daily routine. It is quite a treat in February when the Red-winged Blackbirds invade the Ponderosa Pines of my neighborhood. I'm accustomed to seeing them in marshes, not swaying in the tree tops. Paying attention to "normal" allows us to notice the unusual. So come spring and fall, stand ready. A surprise migrant may be coming to a feeder near you! You can also contact your local center of the National Audubon Society for migratory events in your area.

Promise of Hope

"And the Lord shall guide thee continually, and satisfy thy soul in drought" (Isaiah 58:11, KJV).

On this spiritual journey of life, there will be fog, turbulence, and times of exhaustion. And as weary birds won't fly, flagging souls too are denied. In such times, we must remember to lie down in green pastures; to stop beside quiet waters.

Discussion Guide

Field Work of the Heart, Soul, & Mind

Chapter-by-chapter questions for further discussion as an individual or in a group, keeping in mind this scripture:

"When I look at your heavens, the work of your fingers, the moon and the stars that you have established; what are human beings that you are mindful of them, mortals that you care for them?"
–Psalm 8:3-4, NRSV

1
GRACE SINGS ON CRICKET WINGS

1. What was your favorite childhood pet?

2. Look at the cricket, the work of God's hands, and its ability to make music by drawing the scraper "bow" of one wing against the file "fiddle" of the other wing. Then ask: "Who are we, that he is mindful of us?" How does this view of the cricket enlarge your view of God?

3. Consider the author's statement, "I kept God much as I kept my pet cricket—caged and safely ensconced in my routine, my demands, and my comfort zone." What do we risk losing when we cage God? What do we gain when we unleash his power in our lives?

4. Discuss Matthew 6:6. "Here's what I want you to do: Find a quiet, secluded place so you won't be tempted to role play before God. Just be there as simply and honestly as you can imagine. The focus will shift from you to God, and you will begin to sense his Grace" (*The Message*). Why is it that we tend to role play before others? Before God? How would our lives be different if we were honest about *who we really are*, with each other, with ourselves, and with God?

5. The author shares her struggles in the journey to become who God created her to be. Discuss the importance of being able to shed other people's expectations for your life and pursue God's purposes for your life.

6. What new discovery did you make about the cricket? About yourself?

7. Contemplate one gift you believe God graced you with. Pray for a practical way to use this gift in the coming weeks.

2
SEED, GLORIOUS SEED

1. Describe your dream garden.

2. Look at the seed, the work of God's hands, and its ability to develop into a mature plant from a dormant, dried up bit of life. Then ask: "Who are we, that he is mindful of us?" How does this view of the seed enlarge your view of God?

3. What challenges must a seed overcome to sprout? In what ways does this remind you of the obstacles we must overcome in our own lives? Discuss some of the obstacles Gregor Mendel faced in his life.

4. Read Romans 8:28. The author states that "Life has no wasted experiences." What does she mean by this? Do you agree or disagree? Why?

5. Harvest time: Read Galatians 5:22. List some virtues that have sprouted in your life. Which virtue is still a seedling? Which has grown into a mature plant that has produced fruit? Why is it important that we bear this biblical fruit with our lives?

6. Write down one fruit from Galatians 5:22 you need most in your life today. Ask God to allow the seed of that fruit to develop as you continue to grow in the knowledge of him.

7. Read John 10:10. Jesus says he came so that we might have abundant life. Meditate on some of the blessings in your life. Spend some time in praise and thanksgiving.

8. What new discovery did you make about the seed? About yourself?

3
FLOWER POWER

1. Describe a time you received or gave the gift of flowers. How did it make you feel?

2. Look at the flower, the work of God's hands, and its ability to attract a pollinator with the power (and wonder) of scent and color. Then ask: "Who are we, that he is mindful of us?" How does this view of the flower enlarge your view of God?

3. Read Revelation 4:11. In what ways can the beauty of a flower draw us into worship?

4. The author refers to her need for an "altitude adjustment" when it comes to worship. Describe what she means by this. Is this important? Why or why not?

5. How can community worship with the family of God enrich the faith experience?

6. God's presence is a fact. Worship does not change that. What changes is how we experience his presence. Read Nehemiah 9:5-6. How could taking this scripture to heart improve your worship experience?

7. Read Psalm 46:10. When we rush, how does it affect our ability to worship?

8. What practical steps can you take to make your time with God more meaningful and more glorifying to him?

9. What new discovery did you make about the flower? About yourself?

4
THE LIVES OF LEAVES

1. What's your favorite food?

2. Look at the intricacies of the leaf, the work of God's hands, and its ability to manufacture its own food with sunlight, water, and carbon dioxide. Then ask: "Who are we, that he is mindful of us?" How does this view of the leaf enlarge your view of God?

3. How are leaves important to our existence?

4. In what ways are leaves and prayer similar?

5. Are you more likely to pray first, and then act—or spring into action before praying? Does the order make a difference? How?

6. Why do we tend to shy away from prayer? List a stumbling block to your prayer life and draft a plan to remove it.

7. The author states that prayer "gets us up and over the mountain we thought we could not climb." Describe a time when prayer had the effect of *The Little Engine That Could* in your life.

8. Read Philippians 4:6-7. If we took these words to heart, how would our lives be different? Write down one situation in your life that is causing you anxiety today. Take it to the Lord in prayer.

9. What new discovery did you make about the leaf? About yourself?

5

LEAF SCARS

The Art of Living Scarfully

1. How many physical scars do you have? Which one(s) do you brag about?

2. Look at the leaf scar and its design, the work of God's hands, and its ability to protect the plant from harm after the loss of the leaf. Then ask: "Who are we, that he is mindful of us?" How does this view of the leaf scar enlarge your view of God?

3. The author describes the culprit in leaf fall as "a little rotund donut shaped dude who severed the leaf from its life-giving supply of water and nutrients." This is the beginning of the leaf scar formation. This process seems harmful, yet this scar protects the tree. How?

4. Read Skin Horse's explanation of becoming real from *The Velveteen Rabbit*. Discuss the value of life's scars in helping us become real. In what ways are you becoming more "real?"

5. The topic of pain in our lives is often a difficult subject. Describe a time in your life when pain has brought you closer to God.

6. The author states that the resurrecting of Jesus' body with very real and evident scars served a purpose. Do you agree or disagree? Why or why not? Read 1 Peter 2:24. How have Jesus' scars healed you?

7. What new discovery did you make about the leaf scar? About yourself?

6
BIRD WINGS
Flight, Feathers, & Faith

1. Describe a time you wished you could fly.

2. Look at the feather, the work of God's hands, created with barbs and barbules that hook together and strengthen the feather. Then ask: "Who are we, that he is mindful of us?" How does this view of the feather enlarge your view of God?

3. The author states, "If we are to soar in this life, we would do well to mimic the structure of the feather." What does she mean? Do you agree? Why or why not?

4. The Wright brothers experienced numerous setbacks and failures on their journey to flight success. Share a time in your life when you overcame obstacles to reach your goal.

5. How's your spiritual flight life? Are you grounded? Fluttering and flapping? Gliding and soaring? List some practical ways we can link up to God for sustained flight.

6. According to Ephesians 6: 10-18, where will our strength be found? Consider your armor. As the bird must preen its feathers for maximum efficiency, so we must keep our armor rust free and ready for action. Which piece of your armor needs maintenance? Which piece is shiny and bright?

7. Read Isaiah 40: 28-31. What are we promised if we hope in the Lord? Strive to memorize verse 31.

8. What new discovery did you make about the feather? About yourself?

7
THE DRAGONFLY
Lowlife Larva to Acrobatic Adult

1. Describe someone in your life who has changed for the better.

2. Look at the dragonfly, the work of God's hands, and its ability to transform from the aquatic larval stage into an airborne adult. Then ask: "Who are we, that he is mindful of us?" How does this view of the dragonfly enlarge your view of God?

3. The author describes the life stages of the butterfly: egg, caterpillar (larva), cocoon (dragonflies lack this stage), and adult. What stage of life are you in today? Remember that life is a journey. We are constantly being transformed.

4. Read Acts 9: 1-9. Describe a major change in your life that caused you to ask, "Who are you, Lord?" What did you learn from this experience?

5. Consider the Saul to Paul transformation. Discuss how Christianity would have been different if Saul had not changed. How has his changed life impacted you directly?

6. Read and discuss Ephesians 4:22-24. Why is it important to "molt" our old selves?

7. Write down one attitude or behavior that is "skin tight" and restricts your spiritual growth. Ask God to split this skin of behavior, to free you from this "old way." Be diligent in prayer. "For nothing is impossible with God" (Luke 1:37).

8. What new discovery did you make about the dragonfly? About yourself?

8
BUTTERFLIES
Chasing the Blues

1. What is your favorite color? Why, do you think, is that particular color your favorite?

2. Look at the butterfly wing and its microscopic scales, the work of God's hands, and their ability to reflect light in a rainbow of color. Then ask: "Who are we, that he is mindful of us?" How does this view of the butterfly enlarge your view of God?

3. Every day, light shines into our lives. Which rays do we absorb? The artificial light of the world, in the form of fame and fortune? Or the brilliant life-giving light of God? List practical ways in which we can reflect God's glory and be a light to others.

4. According to the author, "emotional mood monsoons" are a part of life. What is the author's remedy for "mood madness?" Is this a cure or a coping mechanism? Explain your answer.

5. Read Psalm 13. How do verses 1-2 compare with verses 5-6? What role does David's faith play in his expression of confidence? What can we learn from this?

6. Discuss the author's comment: "Remember that God ministers to us where we are. Not just where we want to be." Share a time when you found this to be true.

7. The "butterfly effect" asks the question, "If a butterfly flaps its wings in Brazil, does it cause a tornado in Texas?" Read and discuss Psalm 145. Identify a specific verse that has the potential to trigger a ripple effect of praise in your life. Write it down and place it in a prominent location in your house.

8. What new discovery did you make about the butterfly? About yourself?

9

BEE DIVINE

1. Who had the most chores to do in your family when you were a kid? What were some of yours?

2. Look at the honeybee, the work of God's hands, and its ability to construct the architectural wonder of the comb. Then ask: "Who are we, that he is mindful of us?" How does this view of the honeybee enlarge your view of God?

3. Read the list of tasks a bee performs in its lifetime as shared in the "Help Wanted" ad of the *Honeybee Gazette*. Does this list surprise you? Why or why not? How has this changed your view of the lowly honeybee, if at all?

4. Read and discuss Judges chapter 4. Would you identify Deborah as a queen bee or worker bee? Why?

5. In verses 6-8, who gave the command to Barak and how did Barak respond?

6. Consider some plausible reasons for Barak's response. When you face a difficult, seemingly impossible battle, how do you respond?

7. Read Ephesians 2:10. How has God prepared you for the good works he has given you to do? What tools did he give you?

8. What new discovery did you make about the honeybee? About yourself?

10
HUMMINGBIRDS
A Lesson in Balance

1. If Jesus were coming to your house for lunch today, what is the first thing you would do?

2. Look at the hummingbird, the work of God's hands, and its ability to beat its wings so fast that it sustains a motionless hover, yet how it can also "flip a switch" that lowers its heart rate to a whisper, and achieve complete rest. Then ask: "Who are we, that he is mindful of us?" How does this view of the hummingbird enlarge your view of God?

3. Discuss Albert Einstein's quote on balance.

4. The hummingbird is a bird of balance. It maintains speed and stillness in levels necessary to sustain life. Why is balance important in our own lives?

5. Read Luke 10:41-42. Jesus gently addresses Martha's worried and upset condition. What does Jesus tell Martha in verse 42? Evaluate your workload. Are you focusing on what is better? Discuss.

6. Do you relate more to Mary or to Martha? Discuss what their conversation might have sounded like after Jesus left.

7. What effect does time spent at the feet of Jesus have on your life? On the lives of others?

8. What new discovery did you make about the hummingbird? About yourself?

11
DANCE of the SAND DOLLAR

1. What is your favorite sea creature? Why?

2. Look at the sand dollar, the work of God's hands, and its ability to travel on tiny spines. Then ask: "Who are we, that he is mindful of us?" How does this view of the sand dollar enlarge your view of God?

3. Naturalists are in the business of discovering how nature works. Share one natural wonder you are curious about.

4. Sand dollars can be tossed ashore during a storm. Discuss the life of John Newton and the impact a storm had on his spiritual life.

5. Share a time when God used a storm to get your attention. What was the result?

6. Read about Paul's experience during a monster storm and shipwreck in Acts 27: 13-44. Why was he able to remain calm in a perilous situation? How can you do the same?

7. Read "The Legend of the Sand Dollar." You can find it at http://LegendOfTheSandDollar.com/. In this legend, the markings of a sand dollar symbolize the birth, death, and resurrection of Christ. Discuss the importance of appreciating nature for the added benefit of its ability to direct our focus to God.

8. Read Jesus' words in John 14:27. What gift does he give to us? How can you make this verse a reality in your life?

9. What new discovery did you make about the sand dollar? About yourself?

12

NATURE'S SPARKLERS

Nature's Sparklers

1. During a power outage, are you more likely to: (a) Relax by candlelight and enjoy the experience? (b) Grab a flashlight and check the breaker box? or (c) Fire up the portable generator and banish the blackout?

2. Reflect on Og Mandino's quote. Do you share his viewpoint?

3. Look at the anglerfish, the work of God's hands, and its ability to "fish" the dark depths of the sea with a built in glowing lure. Then ask: "Who are we, that he is mindful of us?" How does this chapter's description of the anglerfish enlarge your view of God?

4. Have you ever seen bioluminescence? If so, describe the experience.

5. The author compares the process of bioluminescence with that of glow sticks. Recall the minute details required for bioluminescence to occur in living organisms. List some other "God orchestrated" details in nature—and in your life—that amaze you.

6. Consider the words of ocean explorer William Beebe when he saw the wonders of the undersea world (in situ) for the first time. Beebe says he experienced a "tremendous wave of emotion, a real appreciation of what was momentarily almost superhuman, cosmic…" How do you think God feels when we express our appreciation to him for his creation?

7. Read Psalm 8. What emotions does the star-filled sky evoke in the psalmist? In you?

8. The author describes the light of God's Word as "Bible-uminescence." How does God's Word light up your life?

9. Reflect on the wisdom of Psalm 119:105.

10. What new discovery did you make about bioluminescence? About yourself?

13
FISH SCALE SCRAPBOOKS

1. Who is the "keeper of memories" in your family?

2. Look at the fish, the work of God's hands, and the intricacy of its scales that reflect its growth history. Then ask: "Who are we, that he is mindful of us?" How does this view of the fish scale enlarge your view of God?

3. Fish scale growth is dependent upon environmental conditions—growth rates are higher in good conditions than poor ones. How does this compare to growth in our spiritual lives?

4. Reflect on the life of Peter, the fisherman. The author describes three growth rings in Peter's life: purpose, potential, and perspective. Which ring do you relate to most? Why?

5. Read Matthew 14. What did Peter see in verse 30 that caused him to sink? Discuss the importance of focus in our lives. Where should our focus be in times of trouble?

6. Discuss the power of "fish farmer God" to grow us through our life experiences.

7. Evaluate your own spiritual growth rings. What conditions caused wide bands of growth? Consider your current growth rates. Are you stagnant and stalled? Or active and growing? List two areas where you would like to see spiritual growth occur in your life. Pray that God will grow you. Then watch out.

8. What new discovery did you make about the fish scale? About yourself?

14

BARNACLES

Built for Adversity

1. Where is your ideal place to live? Why?

2. Look at the barnacle, the work of God's hands, and its ability to endure pounding waves and exposure to the elements. Then ask: "Who are we, that he is mindful of us?" How does this view of the barnacle enlarge your view of God?

3. Discuss the wonder of the barnacle's "Super Glue supreme." Where is the glue gland located on the barnacle? What makes this natural glue so special? Why are medical researchers interested in it?

4. Read Psalm 63. Discuss David's low tide of emotions. What does he seek? Read verse 8. To what does he cling?

5. What do you tend to cling to in times of trouble instead of God? Why do we forget the staying power of God?

6. Share a time you found God to be your rock.

7. List some areas of your life where you could use some barnacle cement. Pray and ask God to give you the tenacity of a barnacle.

8. What new discovery did you make about the barnacle? About yourself?

15

A UNIQUE TWEET

The American Dipper

1. Who made you feel special when you were a child?

2. Look at the American dipper, the work of God's hands, and its remarkable flexible cornea that allows it to see underwater. Then ask: "Who are we, that he is mindful of us?" How does this view of the swimming songbird enlarge your view of God?

3. List three unique features God has gifted the American dipper with that allow him to live in a habitat usually reserved for diving birds. How has God uniquely gifted you?

4. Why do humans strive to fit in with the crowd instead of celebrating their individuality?

5. John Muir's accident in a machine shop caused him to rethink his purpose in life. Describe an unwelcome event in your life that caused you to change the direction of your life.

6. John Muir documented the effect of songbirds on "hard business men and old miners." Researcher Eleanor Ratcliffe plans to conduct a study of the effect of birdsong on moods. From your own experience, how does bird song affect you?

7. Read Psalm 139. Discuss verses 13-14. How can these verses impart a positive self image in an image-conscious world?

8. What new discovery did you make about the American dipper? About yourself?

16
COMFORT ZONES & CADDISFLY HOMES

1. Describe your first home.

2. Look at the caddisfly, the work of God's hands, and its ability to construct a home from bits of debris, and release itself into the river's raging current. Then ask: "Who are we, that he is mindful of us?" How does this view of the caddisfly enlarge your view of God?

3. Read Joshua 1:2. What did the Lord command Joshua to do? Imagine how Joshua felt about this. How do you feel when God gives you a challenge?

4. Why is it so difficult to step out of our comfort zones?

5. Read Joshua 3. Discuss the risks and rewards of stepping into the river at flood stage.

6. Share a time you took a risk for God. What was the outcome?

7. While the caddisfly does not consciously choose to take a risk by releasing his vulnerable body into the river filled with hungry trout, what would the outcome be if he did not let go and leave?

8. Discuss the history of God's faithfulness in your life. Think of past experiences where he brought you through a river at flood stage. Stack up stones of memories and praise God for his faithfulness.

9. What new discovery did you make about the caddisfly? About yourself?

17
SUPERHERO LICHENS

1. Who was your favorite childhood superhero? Why?

2. Look at the lichen, the work of God's hands, and its ability to survive freezing temperatures, split rocks, and restore nutrient-poor soils. Then ask: "Who are we, that he is mindful of us?" How does this view of the lichen enlarge your view of God?

3. Lichens remind us that this is our Father's world. All creation, no matter how small, serves a role in this world. Discuss the impact of lichens on the ecosystem.

4. Beatrix Potter's research proposing a symbiotic relationship within the lichen was rejected by the establishment scientists. Potter turned rejection into redirection and Peter Rabbit was born. Discuss the value of perseverance in pursuing our passion.

5. Symbiosis is a broad term used to describe a long term relationship between species. How would you characterize your relationship with God? Is it serve and take? Or take and take some more?

6. Lichens exist in an intricate relationship—two organisms as one. How is God woven into your life? Is the connection sound, or is God dangling by a thin thread disengaged from your life? How can you strengthen the God connection?

7. Read Ephesians 2:22. God lives within you. Write down a goal that, with God's help, you dream of accomplishing.

8. What new discovery did you make about the lichen? About yourself?

18
BEETLES, TATTOOS & LOVE

1. What's the first thing that comes to mind when you hear the word beetle?

2. Look at the bark beetle, the work of God's hands, and its ability to carve a "cradle" for its young beneath the bark of a tree. Then ask: "Who are we, that he is mindful of us?" How does this view of the bark beetle enlarge your view of God?

3. What crucial role does the bark beetle play in the ecosystem? Before reading this chapter, how did you feel about beetles? How do you feel now?

4. How does a healthy tree protect itself from the bark beetle? What are some of the tools God has given us to protect ourselves in times of trouble?

5. Discuss the concept of God's never failing, all-encompassing love. Read John 3:16. List the ways God demonstrates his love for us.

6. According to 1 John 3:16, how do we know what love is? What does this challenge us to do? Share a practical way you can do this today, and then carry out that plan.

7. Reflect on Isaiah 49:15-16. Cherish the thought that God will not forget us. Visualize your name engraved on God's hands. Give thanks to the creator and sustainer.

8. What new discovery did you make about the bark beetle? About yourself?

19
THE SECRET LIFE of TREES

1. Tell about a tree that holds a special place in your heart.

2. Look at the tree, the work of God's hands, and its ability to produce bark that protects it, cells that nourish it, and roots strong enough to anchor it. Then ask: "Who are we, that he is mindful of us?" How does this view of the tree enlarge your view of God?

3. Read again Joyce Kilmer's poem, "Trees." Reflect on the gift of trees in our lives.

4. The author discusses the potential development of synthetic trees. Discuss the pros and cons of this technology.

5. Discuss Dwight L. Moody's perspective on happiness versus joy. Do you agree or disagree? Why?

6. How is the bark of a tree like happiness? What part of the tree would represent joy?

7. Read Colossians 2:6-7. Discuss the impact of implementing this scripture in your life. List the practical ways you can continue to live in him daily.

8. Read Jeremiah 17:8. Write this verse on a 3 x 5 card and post it in a prominent place in your house. Resolve to live like a tree planted by the water. What is necessary to grow deep spiritual roots?

9. What new discovery did you make about a tree? About yourself?

20
OF TOADS & TRIALS

1. What's your favorite go-to gadget?

2. Look at the spadefoot toad, the work of God's hands, its tiny digging "tool" and its ability to burrow into the ground and survive until the rains return. Then ask: "Who are we, that he is mindful of us?" How does this view of the spadefoot toad enlarge your view of God?

3. When you need to escape the pressures of life, where do you go?

4. United States Army officer Darius Couch took a break from real life and set out on an adventure in the desert. Share a time you took a time out from the demands of your daily routine. What effect did it have on your life?

5. Read 1 Kings 19. What was Elijah's response to Jezebel's death threat? How have unrealistic expectations caused disappointment in your life? How have you handled it?

6. Who joined Elijah in the cave? What did God ask Elijah in verse 9 and again in verse 13? What is the significance of his question?

7. Has God ever told you to go back and face your fears? When you heeded that advice, what was the outcome?

8. Write down a fear you currently face. Add this to your prayer list. Ask God to accompany you on a journey to address your fear.

9. What new discovery did you make about the spadefoot toad? About yourself?

21
THE RESURRECTION PLANT
Roll Up and Dry

1. Are you more likely to run from a fight or engage in it?

2. Look at the resurrection plant, the work of God's hands, and its ability to withstand the desert's heat and drought. Then ask: "Who are we, that he is mindful of us?" How does this view of the resurrection plant enlarge your view of God?

3. Describe a time you were in a desert—either physically or literally.

4. List some characteristics God has given xerophytess to survive the harsh conditions of the desert. How does the "evader" strategy differ from the "endurer?" If you were a plant, into which category would you fit? Why?

5. The author states, "I find that in putting down roots and planting my feet firmly on the ground, I learn trust." Share a time you learned trust through endurance.

6. Jesus called himself "the resurrection and the life." Read John 11:25-26. Do you believe it? How can you demonstrate this belief in your daily life?

7. Read Philippians 3:10. How can we use what we learned from the resurrection plant to encourage us to remain strong in our suffering?

8. What new discovery did you make about the resurrection plant? About yourself?

22
SHOREBIRDS OF THE DESERT

1. What is the farthest distance you have traveled?

2. Look at the shorebird, the work of God's hands, and the ability of this tiny dynamo to migrate thousands of miles. Then ask: "Who are we, that he is mindful of us?" How does this view of the shorebird enlarge your view of God?

3. Read Ralph Waldo Emerson's quote at the beginning of the chapter. What is the value in adopting this attitude toward life?

4. List two things shorebirds do to prepare for migration. How do these actions help them on the journey?

5. Stopover sites are critical on life's journey. How do *you* rest and refuel?

6. The author discusses the importance of a bird's GPS system. List some of the tools God has equipped shorebirds with to find their way. How has he equipped us for our life journey?

7. Read Psalm 84. Discuss verses 5-8. How do these verses apply to our lives? Give specific examples.

8. What new discovery did you make about shorebirds? About yourself?

NOTES

Introduction: Getting Started

1. Gary R. Kremer, *George Washington Carver in His Own Words* (Missouri, University of Missouri, 1991), 143.

1. Richard Louv, *The Nature Principle* (New York, Algonquin Books, 2011), 246.

Chapter One: Grace Sings on Cricket Wings

1. Lang Elliott and Wil Hershberger, *The Songs of Insects* (New York, Houghton Mifflin Company, 2006), 13.

2., 3. May Berenbaum, "Entomological Bandwith" *American Entomlogist*, Winter 2008, http://www.entsoc.org/PDF/Pubs/Periodicals/AE/AE-2008/Winter/buzz.pdf (accessed October 9, 2012).

Chapter Two: Seed, Glorious Seed

1. Adam Gollner, *The Fruit Hunters* (New York, Simon & Schuster, Inc., 2008), 23.

2. Henry D. Thoreau, *Faith in a Seed* (Washington, DC, Island Press, 1993), xvii.

3. Robin Henig, *The Monk in the Garden* (New York: Houghton Mifflin Company, 2000), 18.

4. Ibid., 52.

5. Ibid., 83.

6. Ibid., 171.

Chapter Three: Flower Power

1. Gretchen Scoble and Ann Field, *The Meaning of Flowers*, (San Francisco: Chronicle Books, 1998), 5.

2. Strong, J., S.T.D., LL.D. (2009). *A Concise Dictionary of the Words in the Greek Testament and The Hebrew Bible*. Bellingham, WA: Logos Research Systems, Inc.

3. Jeremy N. Norman, "William Withering and the Purple Foxglove: A Bicentennial Tribute," *Journal of Clinical Pharmacology*, 25, 1985: 479-83.

4. Andy Zubko, ed., *Treasury of Spiritual Wisdom*, (San Diego, California: Blue Dove Press, 1998), 32.

Chapter Four: The Lives of Leaves

1. Watty Piper, The Little Engine that Could (New York: Platt & Munk, 1986)

2. George Mueller, http://bible.org/seriespage/appendix-8-soul-nourishment-first (accessed January 31, 2012).

3. http://www.scribd.com/doc/57005680/British-Tea (accessed February 25, 2012).

Chapter Five: Leaf Scars

1. Robert Krulwich, "Why Leaves Really Fall Off Trees" Krulwich Wonders…An NPR Sciencey Blog, October 30, 2009, http://www.npr.org/templates/story/story.php?storyId=114288700 (accessed February 22, 2012).

2. Margery Williams, *The Velveteen Rabbit* (New York: Random House, 1985).

3. C. S. Lewis, *The Problem of Pain* (New York: Harper Collins, 2001), 105.

4. Kathryn Parsons, "Dr. Paul Brand, CBE," *The Leprosy Mission*, http://www.leprosymission.org.uk/about/about_the_leprosy_mission/brand.aspx (accessed September 6, 2012).

Chapter Six: Bird Wings

1. Thor Hanson, *Feathers: The Evolution of a Natural Miracle* (New York: Basic Books, 2011), 141.

2. David Andrews, "Wings of Fate: The Wright Brothers Drive for Invention" *Common Ground*, (Fall 2003), http.//www.commonground.cr.nps.gov/pdf/c6_Fall_2003_ptl.pdf (accessed 10/18/2011).

3. Tom Crouch, *The Bishop's Boys: A Life of Wilbur and Orville Wright* (New York: W.W. Norton & Company, Inc., 1989), 215.

4. Ibid., 269-270.

Chapter Seven: The Dragonfly

1. Philip Corbet, *Dragonflies Behavior and Ecology of Odonata* (New York: Cornell University Press, 1999), 24.

2. Ibid., 3.

3. Ibid., 208,225.

4. Cary Kerst and Steve Gordon, *Dragonflies and Damselflies of Oregon: A Field Guide* (Corvallis, Oregon: Oregon State University Press, 2011), 13.

Chapter Eight: Chasing the Blues

1. Brian Boyd and Robert Michael Pyle, *Nabakov's Buttertlies* (Beacon Press, 2000), 97.

2. Quoted from *Setting Hearts Aflutter* http://www.physics.org/featuredetail.asp?id=22 (accessed December 18, 2010).

3. Prum, R.O, Quinn, T, & Torres, R.H. (2006) "Anatomically diverse butterfly scales all produce structural colours by coherent scattering." *Journal of Experimental Biology*. 209, 748-765.

4. Carroll E Izard, *The Psychology of Human Emotions* (Springer, 1991), 24-25.

5. Lisa Ann Smith, "Banish a Bad Mood in 15 Minutes" in *Real Simple Magazine*, http://www.realsimple.com/health/mind-mood/emotional-health/banish-a-bad-mood-in-15-minutes-10000001578807/page3.html (accessed January 5, 2011).

6. Glen Packiam, *Butterfly in Brazil* (Tyndale House Publishers, 2007), 19-20.

Chapter Nine: Bee Divine

1. Hilda Ransome, *The Sacred Bee in Ancient Times and Folklore* (New York, Dover, 2004), 28.

2. Ibid., 30.

3. Susan Brackney, *Plan bee*, (New York: Penguin, 2009), 34.

4. Mark Winston, *The Biology of the Honeybee*, (Cambridge, Massachusetts, Harvard University Press, 1987), 81, 83.

5. Murray Hoyt, *The World of Bees*, (New York: Coward Mc Cann, 1965), 99.

6. Thomas Seely, *Bee Democracy*, (Princeton: Princeton University Press, 2010), 6.

7. John Hunter, *A Manual of Bee-Keeping*, originally published: (London: David Bogue, 1879) republished by Bibliolife, LLC, 23.

Chapter Ten: Hummingbirds

1. Alejandro Rico-Guevara and Margaret A. Rubega, "The Hummingbird Tongue is a Fluid Trap, not a Capillary Tube," *Proceedings of the National Academy of Sciences*, Vol. 108, no.23 p, 9356-9360.

2. Quoted in "Hummingbirds Catch Flying Bugs with the Help of Fast-Closing Beaks" *Science Daily*, July 19, 2011, http://www.sciencedaily.com/releases/2011/07/110719121356.htm (accessed March 26,2012).

3. Ibid.

Chapter Eleven: Dance of the Sand Dollar

1. Judges 7: 1-9.

2. 1 Kings 19: 4-5.

3. Matthew 2: 13-14.

4. J.G. Morin, J.E. Kastendiek, A. Harrington & N. Davis, "Organization

and Patterns of Interactions in a Subtidal Sand Community on an Exposed Coast," *Marine Ecology Progress Series*, Vol. 27, November 14, 1985, 163-185.

5. A. Cabanac and J.H. Himmelman, "Directional Movement of the Sand Dollar Echinarachnius parma," *Ophelia*, Vol. 48, June, 1998, 93-102.

6. John Newton, *Out of the Depths* (Grand Rapids, Michigan: Kregel Publications, 2003), 65.

7. Ibid., 66.

8. Ibid., 71.

9. Ibid., 73.

10. Ibid., 124.

11. Jeremy Reynalds, "The 260th Anniversary of Conversion of 'Amazing Grace' Author," ASSIST News Service, March 22, 2008, http://www.assistnews.net/Stories/2008/s08030138.htm (accessed September 14, 2012).

12. Anne Morrow Lindbergh, *Gifts of the Sea* (New York, Random House, 1962), 16.

Chapter Twelve: Nature's Sparklers

1. Vincent Pieribone and David Gruber, *Aglow in the Dark: The Revolutionary Science of Biofluorescence* (Cambridge, Massachusetts: Harvard University Press, 2005), 12.

2. Ibid., 12.

3. Theodore W. Pietsch, *Oceanic Anglerfishes: Extraordinary Diversity in the Deep Sea* (Berkeley and Los Angeles, California: University of California Press, 2009), 229.

4. William Beebe, *Adventuring with Beebe* (New York: Viking Press, 1955), 82.

5. News story "Scientists Discover Bioluminescent 'Green Bombers' from the Deep Sea" *Science Daily*, August 20, 2009, http://www.sciencedaily.com/releases/2009/08/090820161133.htm (accessed April 4, 2012).

Chapter Thirteen: Fish Scale Scrapbooks

1. Nina Stokes, "The Fin Art of Science" *The Science Teacher*, March 2001, 22-24.

Chapter Fourteen: Barnacles

1. Rebecca Stott, "How Mr. Arthrobalanus saved Charles Darwin from Baron Munchausen's Fate" *The Times Higher Education*, March 14, 2003, http://www.timeshighereducation.co.uk/story.asp?storyCode=175339&sectioncode=26 (accessed April 21, 2012).

2. Pat Hagan, "Blistering Barnacles! Glue from Shellfish Mends Broken Bones" *The Daily Mail*, September 5, 2006, http://findarticles.com/p/

news-articles/daily-mail-london-england-the/mi_8002/is_2006_Sept_5/blistering-barnacles-glue-shellfish-mends/ai_n37905654/ (accessed April 21, 2012).

3. Lidita Khandeparker and Arga Chandrashekhar Anil, "Underwater Adhesion: The Barnacle Way" *International Journal of Adhesion and Adhesives*, Volume 27, Issue 2, March 2007, 165-172. http://drs.nio.org/drs/bitstream/2264/227/1/Int_J_Adhesion_Adhesives_27_165.pdf (accessed September 17, 2012).

4. Gail Cleere, "Battling the Barnacle (and other ship-fouling critters)" in Media Releases from *Office of Naval Research*, 2001, www.onr.navy.mil/en/Media-Center/Press-Releases/2001/Battling-the-Barnacle.aspx (accessed September 17, 2012.

Chapter Fifteen: A Unique Tweet

1. Edwin Way Teale, Ed., *The Wilderness World of John Muir*, (New York: Houghton Mifflin, 2001), 147.

2. Robert Hanna, "John Muir's Relative" *Sierra Nevada Virtual Museum*, April, 2006. Podcast www.sierranevadavirtualmuseum.com/sierraCasts/hanna/hanna.swf (accessed April 11, 2012).

3. Gadi Katzir and Howard C. Howland, "Corneal Power and Underwater accommodation in Great Cormorants (Phalacrocorax carbosinensis)" *The Journal of Experimental Biology*, March 1, 2003, Vol. 206, 833-841.

4. Edwin Way Teal, Ed., *The Wilderness World of John Muir*, (New York: Houghton Mifflin, 2001), 54-55.

5. Dennis C. Williams, *God's Wilds: John Muir's Vision of Nature*, (College Station, Texas: Texas A&M University Press, 2002), 4.

6. Ephesians 1:18.

7. Gary Beeler, "Montana Outdoors Portrait: American Dipper" *Montana Outdoors*, http://fwp.mt.gov/mtoutdoors/HTML/articles/portraits/dipper.htm (accessed September 18, 2012).

8. Edwin Way Teal, Ed., *The Wilderness World of John Muir*, (New York: Houghton Mifflin, 2001), 159.

9. Ibid., 151.

10. Ibid., 149.

11. Patrick Barkham, "Scientists to Study Psychological Benefits of Birdsong" *The Guardian*, December 21, 2011. http://www.guardian.co.uk/environment/2011/dec/21/scientists-study-psychological-effects-birdsong/print (accessed September 18, 2012).

Chapter Sixteen: Comfort Zones & Caddisfly Homes

1. Gary LaFontaine, *Caddisflies*, (New York: The Lyons Press, 1981) 17.

2. Kathy Stoudt owns and operates Wildscape Inc., a family founded business specializing in nature crafted jewelry—works of art produced by caddisflies. Check it out at www.wildscape.com

Chapter Seventeen: Superhero Lichens

1. Patricia Lichen, *River-Walking Songbirds & Singing Coyotes*, (Seattle, WA: Sasquatch Books, 2001), 94.

2. Ibid.

3. Gordon Grice, "Lichens: Fungi that have Discovered Agriculture" *Discover Magazine*, January 6, 2010, http://discovermagazine.com/2009/nov/06-lichens-fungi-that-have-discovered-agriculture (accessed September 26, 2012).

4. Linda Lear, *Beatrix Potter: A Life in Nature*, (New York: St Martin's Press, 2007), 125.

Chapter Eighteen: Beetles, Tattoos & Love

1. Arthur Evans and Charles Bellamy, *An Inordinate Fondness for Beetles* (New York: Henry Holt & Company, Inc., 1996), 9.

2. Rudy Scheibner and Stephanie Bailey, "Insect Info" University of Kentucky Department of Entomology http://www.uky.edu/Ag/Entomology/ythfacts/bugfun/trivia.htm (accessed August 29, 2011).

3. Forest Encyclopedia Network http://www.forestencyclopedia.net/p/p1003 (accessed August 29, 2011).

4. Douglas C. Allen, "The Bark Beetles" *NY Forest Owner*, March/April 1994 http://www.dec.ny.gov/docs/lands_forests_pdf/beetles.pdf (accessed August 29, 2011).

5. Jennifer Johnson, "Tattoos of the Cross" *Christianity Today*, March 19, 2009, http://www.christianitytoday.com/ch/bytopic/missionsworldchristianity/tattoosofthecross.html (accessed August 29, 2011).

Chapter Nineteen: The Secret Life of Trees

1. Joyce Kilmer, *Trees & Other Poems*, (Georgia: Cherokee Publishing Company, 1994), 19.

2. Molly Bentley, "Synthetic Trees Could Purify Air" *BBC NEWS*, February 21, 2003, http://news.bbc.co.uk/2/hi/science/nature/2784227.stm (accessed September 24, 2012).

3. Adam Hadhazy, "Power Plants: Artificial Trees That Harvest Sun and Wind to Generate Electricity" *Scientific American*, May 20, 2009, http://www.scientificamerican.com/article.cfm?id=artificial-trees-harvest-sun-and-wind-energy (accessed April 17, 2012).

4. Ibid.

5. Walter Sneader, *Drug Discovery: A History*, (England: Wiley, 2005), 106.

6. Ibid., 106.

7. Rachel Herz, *The Scent of Desire*, (New York: Harper Collins, 2007), xvii.

8. Dwight Moody, quoted in Alan Keiran *Take Charge of Your Destiny*

(Shippensburg, PA: Destiny Images, 2008), 130.
9. Colossians 2:6-7.

Chapter Twenty: Of Toads and Trials
1. Arthur Bragg, *Gnomes of the Night*, (Philadelphia, University of Pennsylvania Press, 1965), 32.
2. Roger Conant, "Zoological Exploration in Mexico-the Route of Lieut. D.N. Couch in 1853" *American Museum Novitates*, (2350):1-14.

Chapter Twenty-One: Shorebirds of the Desert
1. Harold and Alma Moldenke, *Plants of the Bible*, (New York: The Ronald Press Company, 1952), 38.
2. News Release: "Stress Relief: Engineering Rice Plants with Sugar-Producing Gene Helps them Tolerate Drought, Salt and Low Temperatures, Cornell Biologists Resport" *Science Daily*, November 26, 2002, http://www.sciencedaily.com/releases/2002/11/021126072734.htm (accessed May 3, 2012).
3. Louise Jones and Simon McQueen-Mason, "A Role for Expansins in Dehydration and Rehydration of the Resurrection plant Craterostigma plantagineum" *Federation of European Biochemical Societies*, January 20, 2004, https://homes.bio.psu.edu/expansins/reprints/Jones_McQueenMason.pdf (accessed May 3, 2012).

Chapter Twenty-Two: Shorebirds in the Desert
1. Robert Frost, quoted in Edward C. Lathem, ed., *The Poetry of Robert Frost*, (New York: Holt Rinehart and Winston), 225.
2. Joseph R. Jehl, Jr., "Fat Loads and Flightlessness in Wilson's Phalaropes," *The Condor*, 99, May 1997, 538-543.
3. Dominique Maillet and Jean-Michel Weber, "Performance-Enhancing Role of Dietary Fatty Acids in a Long Distance Migrant Shorebird: The Semipalmated Sandpiper," *The Journal of Experimental Biology*, 209, July 15, 2006, http://jeb.biologists.org/content/209/14/2686.abstract (accessed March 14, 2012).
4. Henry Fountain, "A Low-Tech Compass for Arctic Shorebirds: Just Use the Sun," *The New York Times*, January 16, 2001, http://www.nytimes.com/2001/01/16/science/a-low-tech-compass-for-arctic-shorebirds-just-use-the-sun.html?pagewanted=all&src=pm (accessed March 24, 2012).
5. C.S. Lewis, *The Problem of Pain*, (New York: Harper Collins, 2001), 116.
6. John Ortberg, *Love Beyond Reason: Moving God's Love from your Head to Your Heart*, (Grand Rapids, MI: Zondervan, 1998), 113.

About the Author

With a B.S. degree in Marine Biology from Cal State University Long Beach and a M.S. degree in Biology from California State University San Bernardino, Carol O'Casey has spent years in the field—literally—from cataloging plants high in the mountains of Southern California to mucking through mud monitoring shorebirds in Washington. She has taught science to college students and also to sixth graders, and has been published in the *Journal of Field Ornithology* and in the *Journal of Environmental Entomology*. She and her husband, a Christian minister, and their family live in Oregon. Carol's passion is expounding the wonders tucked in the cathedrals of God's wilds. Learn more about Carol by visiting her blog at http://thedivinenatureproject.com/

To order additional copies of *Unwrapping Wonder* visit the publisher's website at www.cladach.com or order through online retailers and bookstores everywhere.